FAYE BROWNLIE / SUSAN CLOSE / LINDA WINGREN

TOMORROW'S CLASSROOM
TODAY

Strategies for creating active readers, writers, and thinkers

HEINEMANN
Portsmouth, NH

© 1990 Pembroke Publishers Limited
528 Hood Road
Markham, Ontario
L3R 3K9

Published in U.S.A. by
Heinemann Educational Books Inc.
361 Hanover Street,
Portsmouth, NH 03801-3959

Library of Congress Cataloging-in-Publication Data

Tomorrow's classroom today: strategies for creating active readers, writers, and thinkers/Faye Brownlie, Susan Close, Linda Wingren.

p.   cm.

Includes bibliographical references.
ISBN 0-435-08550-6

1. Thought and thinking — Study and teaching (Elementary) 2. Teaching. 3. English language — Composition and exercises — Study and teaching (Elementary) I. Close, Susan. II. Wingren, Linda. III. Title.
LB1590.3.B78   1990
872.6'044 — oc20   90-43250 CIP

Editor: Art Hughes
Design: John Zehethofer
Typesetting: Jay Tee Graphics Ltd.

Printed and bound in Canada
9 8 7 6 5 4 3 2 1

Acknowledgments

Our horizons have been expanded by the many people who have helped put our ideas on the page. Thank you, all our advisors. Your coaching, questioning, and editorial comments have been invaluable.

A special thanks is extended to Trish Grainge for her expertise in drama, which developed into collaborative, hands-on practice and to Bob York, Chilliwack school principal for his photography.

Without secretaries Sandi Prunkl and Lynne Barter there would be no book. We are indebted to their skill and patience.

Dedication

To those teachers and students, especially those at home, whose questioning helped us expand our thinking.

Foreword

What are the ingredients needed in a book for teachers about strategies for developing thinking and learning? *Tomorrow's Classroom Today* not only presents us with the ingredients but also invites us into the process of preparing the feast. Teaching and learning strategies actively exemplified in real classroom situations develop our taste for nurturing students toward the goal of becoming sophisticated, independent thinkers. In each strategy the reader views the process through the words of a classroom teacher, description by an enlightened observer, examples from students, and an analysis of the teaching and learning. The strategy is then given in recipe form at the end of each segment as a framework to be personally modified and extended. This is not a cookbook in the traditional sense of prescriptive formula but rather a model for extending one's repertoire in making good instructional decisions both in the active process of teaching and developing long-term goals and plans for student learning.

What makes *Tomorrow's Classroom Today* especially appealing to both novice and experienced teachers is that each strategy is based upon the best of research and reflective practice and modelled to encourage strategic teaching. The focus is on active styles that teach just beyond the child, honoring the child's imagination and sense of wonder. To illustrate this, a variety of different learning styles and multiple forms of literacy are highlighted.

Tomorrow's Classroom Today is a revisioning of the direct instruction model designing the teaching/learning activities in response to children. Teachers shift their focus from planning a lesson to planning for learning. The strategies are based around sound principles of teaching which emphasize that thinking is valued, and the skills and concepts students are being asked to learn are organized into a coherent structure.

The conversations around each strategy encircle and give life to these principles of teaching. *Tomorrow's Classroom Today* is a collaborative experience much like the shared enjoyment of a great meal. "I bid you feast."

Kit Grauer
Coordinator, Principles of Teaching Course
Faculty of Education
University of British Columbia

Contents

1

On the Edge

Our classrooms today reflect thinking and practice which are *On the Edge*. We bridge the best of what we know — active learning, collaboration, reflection, respect for learning preferences — with a set of teaching/learning strategies. Our goal is to nurture all students toward becoming sophisticated, independent thinkers.

The ultimate goal of school reform is "to create institutions where students can learn through interactions with teachers themselves who are always learning. . . . The more complex and higher order the learning, the more it depends on reflection — looking back — and collaboration — looking back with others."

— Lee Shulman, "Teaching alone, learning together: Needed agendas for the new reforms."

"Ideas about teaching and learning can only have meaning in the context of classroom implementation, and it follows that teachers are crucial participants in any research process."

— Jeff Northfield, "They Will Never Be the Same Again", in *Improving the Quality of Teaching and Learning: An Australian Case Study* — The Peel Project, John R. Baird and Ian J. Mitchell, editors.

"Instructional decisions are best made by teachers who conduct research in their own classrooms. They analyze the performance of their students. The classroom becomes a collaborative community of literacy research where teachers and their students have permission to reflect, analyze and problem-solve about instruction."

— Joy Monahan and Beth Hinson, "New Directions in Reading Instruction."

"When teachers teach in a way that affirms students' worth and dignity, students' academic performance improves."

— Scott Willis, "Feeling Good and Doing Well," in *ASCD* Update.

Since the publication of *Reaching for Higher Thought* we have been humbled and honored by the insightful connections offered by students and teachers alike. Their applications and extensions of our strategies have prompted us to present anew our current thinking.

This second collection of strategies is built upon the challenge of moving beyond our best. As practitioners we read extensively, talk, filter our ideas through each other's experiences, and apply our understandings to classrooms. We work with teachers, carefully observing students in the strategic processes, in a variety of contexts, to authentically document student growth and to evaluate the effects of our instructional decisions. The observations fuel directions for new learning for both students and teachers. Sometimes our students work for extended periods on strategy sequences, and sometimes they work on independent applications or inquiry. They need to experience the strategies many times and in many different contexts to be able to internalize and make independent strategic learning decisions. Thus, activities set up to fit in with the curriculum focus offer students opportunities to investigate and use their new learnings.

As teachers build their classroom inquiry around their students, they weave curriculum content carefully together with processes that invite students to construct meaning. Teachers help students to become decision-makers and critical thinkers. They help them to feel that they can contribute and that their ideas make a difference. We see teachers enhancing the joy of learning. We see learners reflecting confidence with their growing competence. They are stepping into each new experience committed, able to communicate, to cooperate, and to show consideration.

Our own learning has expanded. We "feel the responsibility to implement what we know" (Andrews, 1989) and accept the challenge presented by rapid change in the restructuring of schools.

Today, we work toward classrooms which embrace change, classrooms which are inclusive environments welcoming diversity and respecting each student's uniqueness. In these heterogeneous classrooms, individual responses form the base for expanded expression. Prior experience and thought are networked from individual response through small collaborative groups to whole-group interaction, helping each student make connections.

* * *

It may be only a few years later, but learning looks so different. Jana Cohoe's class can see us peeking over their shoulders, watching and listening and jotting down observations — other teachers in there to learn from them, pretty routine really.

An easy tone characterizes the morning activities of this upper primary class. Several students read through their "wolf" duotangs as others take turns talking about themselves from the front of the classroom. One student looks at the walls, hung as they are with a combination of designs by the children, the teacher, and reproductions of western masterpieces. Even the alphabet is printed on birds that stand in varied positions. One girl's eyes scan the hang-ups, the child at the front, the teacher. The observer senses a friendly environment, one that allows for choices. A couple of children huddle over a wolf picture, talking low since another is addressing the class.

The teacher is engaged in her own activities, though responsive in conversational voice when a child requests an exchange with her. Otherwise, she is more noticeable for how she doesn't assume a role that is very directive.

At about ten minutes into the morning she begins to pull a whole class focus toward the corner where wicker sofas and chairs make a talking area they call the reading centre. The children move to arrange themselves on the furniture and floor while looking at the brightly colored strips of yellow and orange waiting near two hula hoops.

The talking tone does not change as the teacher tells the students what she has been thinking as she planned the lesson. They have learned a lot about wolves from books and discussion and videotapes and she wanted a way for them to use the information they had gathered. She has thought of a strategy that might work. She conveys that it is experimental and they will evaluate its usefulness later. To help them recall some facts about wolves, she asks questions. The response is eager as she records their information on *yellow* strips:

Wolves are very strong animals.
They howl.
They run on their toes.

She now asks them to give facts about human beings. Students note that people are mammals. This fact is put on an *orange* strip for people information. More facts are given and recorded with a felt marker. The teacher asks what they would do if they run out of information that they can remember. For wolves, students say they can look in their resource book, and for people, they can just look at their partners. The class disbands to the central area where tables consisting of four desks each become places of furious energy. In some places a pair of students talk together to come up with facts while one does the recording; in others the two record facts and talk aloud as they write. As students run out of the paper strips they help themselves to more from the front of the room. A pile of color soon fans out at every table. The teacher signals a return to the reading centre. The hula hoops are overlapped to form a Venn diagram.

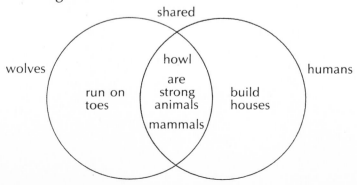

The teacher models how the lesson will develop. An interesting debate arises as to whether 'howling' is a shared characteristic. After the demonstration, groups of four children return to their own areas to decide as a whole group which facts are characteristics of both wolves and people and which are characteristics of just one.

The stage is set for students. The whole-group introduction had taken about ten minutes; the small-group work proceeded through a lively half hour. Each unique formation of four minds was a society in itself. The three observing teachers marveled at the intelligent cooperating they witnessed. Jana knew how to elicit the conditions for it to occur.

What we noticed as different in just a few years is the now familiar and well practised use of many learning strategies, familiar to teacher and students alike, that make learning this active process where it is natural for students to make meaning for themselves. They do so comfortably, surrounded and held by the now confident teacher whose pedagogy is jelling.

The opening of the classroom to other practising and student teachers is *the newer edge*. Teachers' collaborative dialogues based on shared classroom experiences are making for a real professionalism in analyzing, improving, pruning, and rethinking practices.

The teachers thank Jana for extending herself in this way and acknowledge a sense of having seen some good teaching in a classroom which many call a 'classroom of tomorrow'. Jana Cohoe, as a teacher who is familiar with a wide variety of strategies, combines and creates her own to suit her various instructional purposes. In teaming with other practitioners, she is making for herself what she now feels is essential for her students — time and structures within which to learn and reflect collaboratively.

* * *

As you read with us through the following chapters, we invite you to participate in our classrooms, to experiment with your chosen strategies, to design instructional sequences appropriate for your learners, and to craft your teaching in such a way that students grow toward increasing independence as lifelong learners and self-evaluators.

CHILDREN'S BOOKS USED TO SUPPORT STRATEGIES

Bond, Michael. *The Day the Animals Went on Strike.* London: Studio Vista Blue Star House, 1972.

Cleaver, Elizabeth. *The Fire Stealer*. Ojibwa legend retold by William Toye. Toronto: Oxford University Press, 1979.

Khalsa, Dayal Kaur. *I Want a Dog*. Montreal, Quebec: Tundra Books, 1987.

Lester, Helen. *Tacky the Penguin*. Boston: Houghton Mifflin, 1988.

Lunn, Janet and Kim LaFave. *Amos's Sweater*. Vancouver, B.C.: Douglas and MacIntyre, 1988.

Tejima, Keizaburo. *The Bear's Autumn*. La Jola, California: The Green Tiger Press, 1986.

2

Strategic Teaching

Strategic Teaching involves more than just enhancing one's repertoire of strategies. Consideration must also be given to the ongoing instructional decisions made minute-by-minute in the classroom and to long-term strategic planning. This planning includes the context of students, parents, and the school, guiding students toward independent application of the thinking behind the strategies, and one's choice of the strategies in an instructional sequence.

"If teachers are to create classroom communities in which students learn through active, collaborative inquiry, they must have similar learning opportunities themselves."

— Gordon Wells, foreword to *Teachers and Research: Language Learning in the Classroom*, Gay Su Pinnell and Myna L. Matlin, editors.

"If we accept the right to be instructional decision-makers in our own classrooms, we also can accept the responsibility of making good decisions — decisions that enhance student learning, decisions that are born out of reflective practice."

— Faye Brownlie, "The Door Is Open. Won't You Come In?," in *Opening the Door to Classroom Research*, Mary W. Olson, editor.

"Students who receive good strategy training during their years in school can acquire a form of knowledge especially useful in coping with the wide variety of learning situations they will encounter throughout their lives."

— Sharon Derry, "Putting Learning Strategies to Work," in *Educational Leadership*.

". . . a literacy of thoughtfulness is primarily a process of making meaning (not just receiving it) and negotiating it with others (not just thinking alone)."

— Rexford Brown, "Schooling and Thoughtfulness," in *Basic Education*.

Change has many facets. As we work at designing our classrooms for optimum learning for all students, we consider thinking to be the scaffold which supports all of our decisions. We work to engage our learners in actively constructing meaning, in linking prior knowledge to new information, in critically using a set of strategies to understand text, and in reflecting on our actions. Since we are all learners, these tenets apply to students and teachers alike.

THE ORGANIZER

We have developed a frame which guides our introduction and application of each new strategy.

SETTING THE STAGE
1. Identify the strategy to be taught.
2. Discuss the reasons why it is being taught.
3. Tell the steps of the strategy.

MODELING AND DIRECT INSTRUCTION
4. Teach the strategy in an appropriate context.
5. Provide opportunities for whole-group work, collaborative group work, and individual work.
6. Reflect with your students on what you did and why.

GUIDING PRACTICE
7. Review the steps of the strategy with the students.
8. Establish criteria for effective use of the strategy.
9. Use the strategy in a variety of contexts and with a variety of texts.
10. Reflect with the students on their growing competency with the strategy.

ENCOURAGING INDEPENDENT APPLICATION
11. Provide opportunities for students to use the strategy independently in materials of their own choosing.
12. Encourage adaptation of the strategy to fit text, context, and personal style.
13. Monitor the students' expertise and independent application of the strategy.
14. Monitor the gradual diminishment of teacher support needed.

As students and teachers integrate a new strategy into their repertoire, they begin to adapt the original form into one which more closely matches their learning/teaching goals and styles. This is the measure of lifelong learning. It reflects a movement through the stage of learning when one is acquiring a foundation of knowledge to the stage where one is generating knowledge, adapting and changing the strategy to fit new learning situations as they arise.

Gill Bickerton of Langley is such a strategic teacher. Initially, Gill was using new strategies in an attempt to increase her strategic repertoire. She attended workshops, read extensively, practised with her students, and reflected on the learning she saw happening. As her expertise developed she decided to adapt some of the strategies to better fit her students' learning needs and her personal talents as a teacher.

Since Gill had experienced the fruits of collaborative planning, she invited Daphne Stevens to plan with her. They chose to adapt the strategy **Sort and Predict** for an early primary audience. Rather than choose key concept words from the text, Gill and Daphne drew eight pictures which reflected story characters and story elements. They arranged their children in groups of three and had them sort their pictures into groups of beginning, middle and end, talking together as they sorted. This was followed by individual

writing on "What can this story be about?" The children shared their writing in their small groups, then with the class. Vocabulary was now introduced, using a pocket chart and matching the words with the pictures. Since this activity generated so many more predictions, the children talked again about what they knew now. Finally, she read the story *Amos's Sweater* by Janet Lunn and Kim LaFave.

The following day, the children represented their understanding of the story at a variety of centres. Their choices included acting out the storyline, written retellings, plasticene models, and paintings of Amos's sweater. The children really enjoyed participating in this form of **Sort and Predict** and remembered a great deal in their retellings.

The teachers were also enthusiastic with these results, and so played with further adaptions. With *Tacky the Penguin*, by Helen Lester, the children sorted the pictures three times, sharing their classifications as a class after each sorting: first, in two categories; second, in two different categories; third, using four pictures for a story beginning, and then placing the remaining pictures in sequence and creating a story from these prompts.

Gill and Daphne found that when they added a blank picture frame and encouraged the children to draw in it, their ownership of their story increased. The more these teachers and students work with this strategy, the more easily they change it to fit the purpose of the lesson and the learning needs of the participants. Notice that the focus is on one strategy at a time as the teachers concentrate on implementation and personalization.

PLANNING THE DAY

Most of our strategies require a 90-minute time frame. Since this is an intense teaching/learning period, effective time-tabling should structure students into a less rigorous learning activity after a strategy session.

The strategy sequence does not replace daily personal reading and writing. Because most of the strategies focus on *shared* reading and writing experiences, students still require *daily, personal* practice in reading books of their own choice and designing individually appropriate responses to their reading. These choices often spring from the shared experience and thus are integrated into the learning sequence. This independent reading/writing time is an opportunity for teachers to collect data on independent learning behaviors, to listen to individual children read, and to conference with them on their reading and writing.

CREATING INDEPENDENT LEARNERS

Phyllis Bowman of Vernon has been recording growth in independent application of strategies with her primary class. In November, Phyllis taught **Thinking Bubbles**. In the spring, she called to tell us how excited she was with her students' application of this strategy.

Each morning the children enter the class, pick up their 'Thought Books' and without teacher direction, begin writing or sketching what is on their minds. One of the most frequently used forms of expression is thought bubbles with inside/outside voices.

This independent application of a strategy is our goal. As we observe students choosing to apply the processes which have been taught, we have evidence that they are more enabled learners.

CHOOSING A STRATEGY

Many researchers link their observations to three phases of a lesson in describing the teaching of reading: 'pre', 'during', and 'post'. We spend a large proportion of our time in the pre-reading phase, activating prior knowledge, predicting, questioning, writing to learn, and building from oral language and images. The focus of the 'pre' and the 'during' reading phase is on strategies which develop thinking. In 'post' reading, students frequently learn to write or explore various ways of representing thinking as we move toward strategies which shape thought to form.

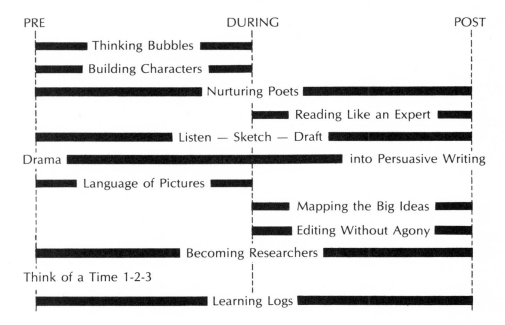

IN THE SCHOOL

In some staff development programs, teachers choose to focus on a new strategy every six weeks. All teachers in the school learn the same strategy in an in-service, demonstration, practice, and reflection cycle. As with student learning, we dig for deeper understanding rather than dance through knowledge as we polish our practice over time.

At Stoney Creek Community School in Burnaby, Donna Woolliams and her staff formed Resource Teams to address student learning needs. Special education teachers were part of these teams as the school had full integration of all special needs students.

Teacher collaboration has led to team teaching, multi-age classes, and even a redefinition of learning for the staff! The teachers frequently observe in each other's classrooms and mentor one another, providing support, advice, and consultation. As collaborators they have moved beyond the lamination of the strategies to critical reflection on practice over time and ongoing refinement of instructional skill.

It has truly become a community of learners and a thinking school. Donna reports that this foundation of school climate enabled her staff to focus on thinking strategies and cooperative learning in a risk-free environment — the glue that holds it all together.

INFORMING PARENTS

Parents are always their children's first teachers and are therefore invaluable as partners in the learning/teaching process. Thus they need to be kept informed of our changes and given guidance in how best to support their children's learning.

Teaching in Shelly Creelman's Grade 3 class looks and sounds differently today from what it did when many of her students' parents were in the school. To help them keep pace, Shelley sends home a monthly newsletter, highlighting what she values in student learning.

DEAR PARENT OR GUARDIAN:

We are sending home our Chinese Learning Logs and our Lantern Books which show evidence of skill development. Please look at the work they are bringing home to share with you, in terms of the thinking and 'real' learning they are achieving.

The Lantern Book is a DRAFT (i.e., spelling was not the major objective; rather it was to be able to use their field notes, lists, webs, etc. to write a 'journal' entry). The purpose of the Learning Log and Lantern Book then becomes a guide for discussion between you and your child so he or she can tell you much more about each experience, not just what was written. Being able to speak about experiences is a necessary skill for children to develop. Thank you for taking the time to read this lengthy note (I got carried away) and THANK YOU for realizing that feedback and encouragement from you is the first and foremost meaningful reward for your child.

Shelly Creelman
Walton Elementary School

Together, in partnerships, we seek to create learning environments which spark the young "Adams" of our world to speak with confidence. (Our Adam is six years old.)

Name Adam
(6 years)

3

Thinking Bubbles: Using Projective Language in Reading Like a Writer

The *Thinking Box* strategy invites students into the minds of story characters and has them represent their thinking in cartoon illustrations using the inside and outside voices of the characters. The teacher reads the text to the students and stops three or four times to have them 'show me what's happening'. This has been a popular and powerful strategy for students of all ages.

"Because the goal is independence, moving beyond self-correcting into self-regulating behavior, it is the teacher's job to help make the student aware of strategies he is using."

— Regie Routman, *Transitions.*

". . . if children's efforts are valued only as writing, we may look for evidence of child creativity that fits the conventions of the writing process and of written language narratives. And we may thus fail to understand what, in fact, the children are doing."

— Anne Haas Dyson, "The Imaginary Worlds of Childhood: A Multimedia Presentation."

"Teachers can gather data systematically while teaching, and students can self-assess actively while learning. Teachers can respond immediately to the data gathered while students become informed partners in their learning."

— Carol S. Brown and Susan L. Lytle, "Merging Assessment and Instruction: Protocols in the Classroom."

". . . consciously generating . . . parts of a thought: the mental pictures, linguistic information, sensory information and feelings. It is actively creating experiences for each of the different aspects of a thought."

— Robert J. Marzano and Daisy E. Arrendondo, *Tactics for Thinking.*

TEACHER: Today we are going to adapt a strategy you have used many times, **Reading Like a Writer**. To begin, fold your paper into four boxes. These will be your thinking boxes. I am going to read a story with you, stopping four times. Each time I stop, I will ask you to 'show me what's happening' in the story and to 'think like the characters'. How many of you read cartoons?

Hands shot up in this combined Grade 4/5 class as I settled in to observe the introduction of a new strategy. As usual, I was impressed with the attentive behavior of the students and their keen desire to acquire a new tool. For this lesson, I had chosen to focus on two students in particular — one described as quiet and less thoughtful; the other, as a powerful and reflective thinker.

New information, including process information, is linked to what is known.

TEACHER: How does a cartoonist indicate that someone is speaking?

How does a cartoonist indicate that someone is thinking about something, or using one's inside voice?

Have you noticed that sometimes you can say one thing and think something else? Think for a moment of a time when your outside voice said one thing and your inside voice said another. Turn to your partner and tell your story of inside/outside voices.

Students are encouraged to find a personal connection to inner/outer dialogue. Sharing their own story gives an oral rehearsal to all and provides an audience for a personal event. Thus all begin the strategy from a 'can do' stance.

All were participating, eagerly exchanging their stories of when they had said one thing and really thought something else. Their conversations lasted about four minutes.

TEACHER: Did you hear something that surprised you? That made you smile? That made you think of a similar experience that you had had? My story today is actually a legend that is retold by William Toye and illustrated by Elizabeth Cleaver, called *The Fire Stealer*. What do you know about legends?

The teacher's role is to model and extend the conversations in positive directions.

STUDENTS: They aren't true.

They are like myths — old stories about people.

They were made up when people didn't know very much science.

Students share current knowledge of the genre to begin a frame for understanding and for expectation.

It's an old story cast down from generations.

They are about Indians.

TEACHER: That is quite a lot of information. I would add that this legend explains an event in history. Do you have any predictions about this legend, *The Fire Stealer*, or about what the event might be?

STUDENTS: This might be when the Indians first got fire.

It might be about someone stealing the Olympic torch.

The guy could be a hawk and pick it up with his claws and fly off.

TEACHER: Well, let's see. As I begin to read, be thinking about the setting of this legend and about what the characters could be thinking and feeling.

The students settled back in their seats ready to confirm their predictions. The teacher read the first part of the legend, a legend of Nanabozho, the creator-magician of the Ojibwa, stopping after Nanabozho had turned himself into a tree to fool his friend.

TEACHER: In your first thinking box, please show me what is happening. Remember to think like a cartoonist and try and use both inside and outside voices for your characters.

A hush fell over the class as the students began their interpretation of what had happened thus far in the legend. No explicit mention had been made of drawing, yet most began with a sketch. They worked almost silently for five minutes.

TEACHER: I would like you to share what you have completed so far in your groups of four. Don't worry if you are not quite done. As you are sharing, notice what others have done in their thinking box that surprises you.

Again about five minutes was taken up with student sharing. There seemed to be no difficulty in keeping these students on task.

TEACHER: What did you notice that people had done differently?

STUDENTS: Jeremy used more than one thinking bubble for Nanabozho.

Dennis had his guys thinking in PICTURES. I never thought of pictures. I only used words.

Faustine made the whole woods, not just one tree.

TEACHER: Wow! Look at the range of choices you have. You can use a series of speech or thinking bubbles, think in words, pictures, or maybe even symbols, or work in story elements and setting with the background in your thinking box. Let's continue and see what happens to Nanabozho. Do you think he will stay as a tree?

As she resumed her reading, a few students continued working on their thinking boxes. They were not stopped by the teacher, as they continued to polish their thinking. This time she stopped once the legend's problem had been posed, and a solution suggested — Nanabozho needed fire to cook food for his grandmother, Nokomis. He could steal it from the warrior who was guarding the torch.

TEACHER: In your second thinking box, show me what's happening. Be sure to borrow any of the ideas you heard or saw. Try also to really think like the characters and show what is going on inside their heads. You may want to show both Nanabozho and his grandmother, Nokomis.

The same process of individual interpretation, sharing in the group of four, and total class ''special interest'' occurred. The students seemed even freer in their constructions this time and used language from the text in their speaking and thinking bubbles. Students did not seem inhibited by the wide variety of artistic renderings, nor did they pay much attention to one another as they began their work. They were surprisingly skilled at explaining to each other the thinking and planning they had undergone in the creation of their thinking boxes.

TEACHER: I noticed something new this time. I observed a student using speaking bubbles within thinking bubbles. Someone was thinking about someone speaking. I also noticed that you are using very specific language both from the text and from your own background information. I am impressed with how clear and precise you are in showing me that you really understand this legend. Let's go for one more segment.

The third thinking box started after a journey. Nanabozho had arrived at the wigwam of the warrior who had stolen the fire and needed a plan to get inside the tent, past the warrior and his daughter, and steal the fire back. Several events had occurred during this segment.

STUDENTS: This is really hard this time because there is so much to show.

You can make more than one thing happen in your thinking box, you know. You just have to make it like time passing.

The teacher consolidates and reiterates student choices without isolating individuals.

Use of time is flexible. Students stop drawing when they have a sense of completion.

Learning from one another is respected and encouraged.

Gentle reminders are given as suggestions.

Students relax into the activity and become freer in redesigning information from the story.

The teacher models learning as a blend of experience and text.

Reading a longer segment allows students to focus on the event which 'most struck them' OR on a means of presenting a series of events.

I showed inside and outside the wigwam, like inside and outside your head.

Yeah, that's a good idea.

TEACHER: Have you noticed that what you are doing in your thinking boxes is just like creating your own mind's movie of the legend? I would expect that this strategy will really help you remember the story because you have recreated it as we have been reading. I am pleased to see that you are seriously adopting different language and thinking for different characters. That is quite a sophisticated skill. Shall we read on and see if the fire does make it home to the village? If it does, do you think the Indians will value it this time or fear it?

She models the predictions which fuel her own reading.

She finished reading the text, and the students completed their thinking papers. They had been working and learning together for an hour and 15 minutes, quite a long time to process a relatively short piece of text! The students, however, were obviously highly engaged and unaware of the time passing.

TEACHER: Before we finish today, I would like to take a few moments to reflect on what we did in this strategy and why we did it. You will recall, of course, that I always believe you can use the thinking we do together when you are working independently. In your learning logs, jot down what comes to your mind about the what and why of today's strategy.

Reflection encourages personal adoption of the strategy as students gain ownership and conscious control.

STUDENTS: I noticed that an author must really know what he's writing about so the illustrator can do a good picture.

I like being able to draw instead of just writing all the time.

I like the way you make boring stories interesting.

This will remind me of how they brought fire to the trees.

I'll probably remember this forever!

I helped collect the students' thinking papers. Two of the boxes of the 'quiet, less thoughtful' student follow. Dennis (nine years old) had been very quiet throughout the lesson. His sketches demonstrate, however, that he is not necessarily less thoughtful, but is, perhaps, differently thoughtful. He used very little language, but demonstrated understanding in sophisticated sketches. He was the first to use thinking bubbles within thinking bubbles, pictures in his thinking bubbles, or a series of events within one box — including a transformation scene! I was again reminded of how conscious we must be of including opportunities for students to represent their understandings in a variety of ways.

Students who are less fluent language users can flourish when demonstrating their comprehension in less language dependent ways.

The powerful and reflective thinker (also nine years old) had been
verbal throughout the lesson. His projections follow — perceptive and
detailed, as expected.

Because this strategy focused on personally negotiated interpretations of text, the needs of the spectrum of abilities had been ably addressed. Students wove together their experiences, the story of the legend, and a personal design.

Extensions

With longer text, teachers have used **Thinking Boxes** to retell a chapter or to capture a special moment from a chapter. This can also be linked to predictions that a student has for the next chapter. As a final activity, students reflect on this strategy as a means of increasing one's enjoyment of a novel.

Student Response Sheet

Strategy: Retelling and Predicting

Name: _____ Date: _____

Retelling	Prediction
	Mrs. Frisby is frightened. She thinks Jeremy will stop flying. He is just gliding. The come to the owl's home. Mrs Frisby is frightened. When Mrs. Frisby says she is Jonathans widower, the owl agrees to help her.
	When they land on the branch, Mrs. Frisby is reluctant to go inside the hole in the tree where the owl lives. She does not trust owls. She could refuse to see the owl because she would be so frightened Then she may never get the owl's help. Besides the hole looked too forbilding. What if the owl trapped her in it and ate her. There would be noone to look after the children.
	When I think now I think more about feelings. It is even more like I am actually living the story. This way really teaches you to think about the actual atmosphere of the story. You can think about all of your feelings. You look at all angles of the story.

THINKING BOXES — RECIPE

1. Review with the students different ways of showing internal and external voices in cartoons.

2. Have the students fold a paper in half twice.

3. Read the selection to the students. Stop at an appropriate spot, once the setting has been established and the characters have been introduced.

4. Instruct the students to:
   "Show what is happening."
   "Think like an illustrator or a cartoonist."
   "Use the inside voice and the outside voice of the characters."

5. Have the students share in pairs or quads.

6. Call attention to surprises the students have shown, such as thinking in pictures, thinking one thing and saying something else, using the author's language.

7. Continue in this fashion for all four thinking boxes.

8. Have the students reflect in writing on what they noticed about their thinking.

9. Have the students retell the story.

10. Process with the students how this strategy helped them remember the story by thinking like the characters.

4

Building Characters

Constructing character predictions from artifacts and language of the text prior to reading greatly increases motivation to read and comprehension during reading. In *Building Characters*, students work collaboratively to weave meaningful connections from the character evidence. Almost automatically, stories grow from the student conversations about the story characters. Students read independently for confirmation of their predictions.

"We learn most easily when we already know enough to have organizing schemas that we can use to interpret and elaborate upon new information."

— Lauren B. Resnick and Leopold E. Klopfer, "Toward the Thinking Curriculum: An Overview," in *Toward the Thinking Curriculum: Current Cognitive Research*, Lauren B. Resnick and Leopold E. Klopfer, editors.

"Unless individuals develop strategies, as readers, for constructing and critically evaluating their own interpretations of texts and, as writers, for using the texts they create to develop and clarify their understanding of the topics about which they write, they remain dependent on others to do their thinking for them."

— Gordon Wells, "Creating the Conditions to Encourage Literate Thinking", in *Educational Leadership*.

"Data in that study showed that first through sixth-grade children's progress in writing fiction could be traced through their development of characters. . . . Characters become more distinctive as children increase their understanding of the fiction they read."

— Donald H. Graves, "Research Currents: When Children Respond to Fiction," in *Language Arts*.

"When children belong to a classroom community of inquiry that is thoughtful and considerate, they are likely to become thoughtful and considerate themselves. . . ."

— Ron Brandt, "On Philosophy in the Curriculum: A Conversation with Matthew Lipman", in *Educational Leadership*.

The 28 Grade 5 and 6 students were arranged in two concentric semi-circles. They had come to anticipate eagerly the presentation of a new strategy. This was such a day.

TEACHER: I'm going to give you a brief overview of our new strategy. We will work in groups of three with one information sheet per group. On this sheet are 11 pieces of text taken from a story we will read later. All of the information pieces are about two characters in a story. You will notice that some of the excerpts are direct speech, while others are description. The two characters' names are Hulk and Matt. You are to cut, organize, and predict from the sentences to see if you can get an idea of what the characters are like. Do you have any expectations of who Hulk might be?

STUDENTS: Someone from a movie?

I think Hulk is actually Matt.

Is it Hulk Hogan, the wrestler?

The heavyweight champion?

Respectful of each response, she left a pause that gave everyone 'thinking room'. Her style never seemed to rush students, yet the pace moved to keep all interested.

TEACHER: Who can review for us what the task is this morning?

Several hands shot up and a clear understanding was established. The teacher added a new suggestion.

TEACHER: You may also want to cluster as you work on these characters, getting ideas from the clues and adding your own ideas of what the characters are like. I'll give you 30 seconds to form your groups, working in twos and threes. Are you ready?

The students moved to various locations about the room and began cutting the groups of sentences prepared by the teacher.

TEACHER: Now, I'm going to give you ten minutes. When I clap my hands we'll stop to evaluate whether we need more time. You'll need only one piece of paper to write on. Later, I'll ask you to notice what ideas came to your mind as you talked together.

Students continued and finished cutting the strips, reading in all sorts of funny positions, relaxed and concentrated. The talk was focused and these older students appeared to enjoy the activity of sorting and moving the strips around.

The teacher circulated, stopping to listen in and ask group members to talk about what they were thinking and doing.

Teachers use alternate room arrangements for whole-group instruction.

Students are forewarned of the teaching plan.

This was a deliberate opening to link prior expectations associated with the name 'Hulk'.

Learners share the responsibility for reconstructing the plan. This feedback is necessary to validate student understanding of the task.

Well-known strategies are used in new ways.

At times, students choose their own groups and their optimum learning spaces. These independent choices have grown from more teacher-directed experiences.

In cooperative learning terms, this resource is called interdependence.

Much data on individual students participating in collaborative groups is collected from teacher-student conversations 'in process'.

STUDENTS: First, we read the sentences out loud. We all said what character we thought each sentence belonged to. Sometimes we didn't all think the same, so we had to sort of convince one another [nods] by saying what made sense.

We read one that said, 'a roll of fat jiggled around his waist' and we knew Hulk would be big. We figured out that Hulk was strong also. Then we put aside sentences for Matt. We considered that he might have wanted to commit suicide because he was planning to walk over a river. A river that no one else would walk over. Everyone knew it was a bad time of year to do it.

We found one really hard to fit because they were both talking and it had some confusing sentences in it. We decided it went under Matt when it said, 'I'm not a murderer.'

Student reflective talk on the learning process is encouraged.

Students are becoming aware of the challenge of learning.

Whole-group sharing extends the choices for individual students.

The teacher clapped as planned, bringing a group focus.

TEACHER: Has anyone drawn any conclusions about the story?

STUDENTS: Hulk rules with an iron hand.

It's over a river on a bridge.

TEACHER: What's your evidence?

STUDENTS: Well, it said 'Hero at Dead Man's Bridge' and it said he shouldn't have been near the river.

Students are pushed to explicitly weave together prior knowledge and text support.

TEACHER: Any more conclusions?

STUDENT: I have a prediction. I predict that Hulk is going to fall in the water and Matt is going to save him.

TEACHER: What makes you think that?

STUDENT: Well, because Matt wouldn't have a choice. The river's wild but he couldn't be a sissy.

TEACHER: Hmm. You are using your text evidence well. I'll give you another five minutes to consolidate your thinking. You should have two groups of information sorted and one cluster about each — ideas, questions, predictions.

The teacher models strategies of good readers and thinkers.

As she continued touring the groups, she noticed two students who had arranged the strips to form a storyline. One signalled to her.

STUDENTS: We think we know what's going on. What we think is so far there's a bridge. Hulk falls in and Matt saves him heroically.

We said that because of where we read 'Hero at Dead Man's Bridge'. 'Hero' made us think, well, it'll be one of them 'cause you'd pick main characters to start us off. Otherwise it would be a wild goose chase if you picked unimportant people.

Students are keen to air their connections.

She smiled in appreciation of the candor of these two, the latter always pushing to create challenges for himself at every opportunity, pulling his less animated classmate along.

These clusters were in process as she peered into a huddle of two Grade 6s and one Grade 5.

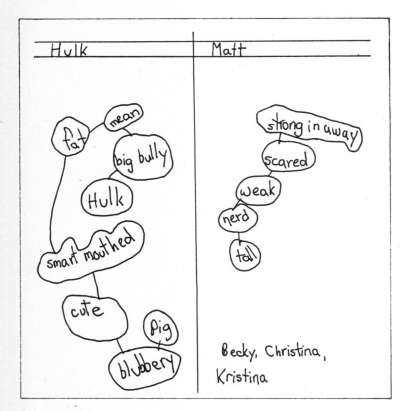

STUDENTS: I think Hulk's a big-mouthed bully. And that he's going to tell Matt he's a wimp. He talks kind of smart-mouthed and he's fat and throws his weight around. He kind of walks mean even and leans against posts or rails. Or if he had straw, you know, he'd sort of chew it hanging out of the corner of his mouth.

He looks like he thinks he's smart and cute. Really he's a kind of pig.

We thought he was all blubbery too. He talks too much and tries to scare Matt with his talk.

At first Matt seemed like he'd be tall and weak, kind of a nerd, scared of Hulk. But then we thought maybe he was strong in a way.

In other words, Matt is a superficial 'sitcom' type of characterization.

TEACHER: How did you arrive at that conclusion?

STUDENTS: When we decided that Hulk was going to lose his balance and fall in, we thought Matt would save him. But he'd tell Hulk to stop bugging him from now on — like that was the condition for saving him.

And he stuck to it. Maybe Hulk was sinking in the water and Matt was holding out for his terms, for Hulk to get off his case and stay off it.

That's good. We didn't say that before — not just like that. I can just see Hulk going down for the last time doing a help sign.

Quiet probing and verbaliza-
tion to another audience
deepens student connections
and clarifies their thinking.

Maybe if he was so fat he'd float up.

Well, it doesn't fit here.

Maybe they'll become friends. Hulk may change after he sees his whole miserable life flash by when he's under water that last time.

What about them being real good friends?

Yeah, Matt could coach Hulk in wrestling and Hulk could become a famous star.

And Matt could teach him how to swim when he wasn't wrestling.

The group had gone the gamut of emotions ending at friendship for the main characters, having only minutes before begun with an exaggerated meanness and timidity. They seemed to arrive at places where both characters were in their own ways both strong and weak. Their talk had most certainly blown the characters into multi-dimensional creatures rather like themselves.

TEACHER: Please take a separate piece of paper that doesn't have character notes on it. You need to change channels in your brain. Review what you did. You were asked to make connections. That's what your brains automatically do, especially when you chat and argue about possibilities. For three minutes I'm going to ask you to look back in, to analyze how your brain was working over the last while as you did these activities. What was going on for you?

Individual reflection places
students in more direct control of their own learning.

Silence reigned as the children stopped to write wherever they were in the room. They were familiar with using writing to comment on their thinking.

SAMPLE 1

When we were clustering and sorting with each other I found that my brain was a cluster of different things. One of those things was on a prediction. I had the whole thing memorized in my brain and couldn't wait to blurt it out. Another thing I had my mind set on was the cluster I had all these words but I didn't know where to start. I think I thought and talked about the prediction the most.

— Kristina (11 years)

SAMPLE 2

My brain tried to make everything fit together as a story. And it also made me hear me and my partner only. I thought about Matt and the paragraph I got out of his sentences.

— Jason (11 years)

SAMPLE 3

My group was Kristina and Becky. We sorted some words and clustered about two characters: Hulk and Matt. In this exercise we concentrated on making predictions or hypotheses about what would happen next. We didn't do much on our cluster, but we sure enjoyed predicting. After the process, Mrs. Wingren interviewed us. We thought mostly about our predictions. We fought a lot about them. But we finally agreed on one thing.

— Christina (11 years)

Student interviews provide a great deal of information to fuel further instruction.

TEACHER: What did you focus on?

STUDENTS: We had to agree on what color Hulk and Matt were. We kept coming back to that.

Our group predicted mostly.

We tried to get a picture of the two characters by adding what we all thought.

Responses focus on what was personally most meaningful — individual connections and participation or on group functioning.

TEACHER: So you were building in details. [nods] How many of you thought there would be a challenge?

STUDENTS: Yeah, we thought a fight or a race.

I have a different prediction. I thought Hulk challenges Matt to walk the bridge and Matt chickens out, so Hulk shows him.

TEACHER: So you think Hulk is the hero?

STUDENT: We weren't too sure.

TEACHER: Who thinks someone else will be the hero?

A few hands respond.

TEACHER: Begin to read the story I've passed to your group. You may read however you choose: one can read or you can take turns or read silently.

The students chose once again to collaborate. No group copied another. The reading arrangements were fashioned after the personalities in the group. What was common to all, however, was the energy they brought to their reading. All the predicting and building of characters had fed their curiosity.

In one group a shy, good reader was seen reading aloud to the usually more extroverted partner who experienced print as a difficult medium. Cory appeared quiet and studious here as if his partner's smooth reading was satisfying a deep need to know what was going on between Hulk and Matt, something which would have taken him eons to decipher for himself. One had the feeling that their exchange drew a balance — one needed to be heard, the other to learn to listen. Asked later if the work before the reading was useful, even though the predictions were pretty far off, Cory noted, "Most definitely!"

STUDENT: Yes. It made me want to read the story when it said he shouldn't go there. You knew it would be exciting. Also I wondered if our ideas about Hulk and Matt were at all like the author's.

Reading is a negotiation between reader and writer.

TEACHER: Were they?

STUDENT: Some were. Some weren't. [smiles]

This class of confident language users merely saw the author's version as a variation on their own many storylines. Some even remarked that they wouldn't have ended the short story as the author did. They could certainly be termed active, critical readers for whom print has been demystified!

Motivation and comprehension deepen when students are actively involved in personally constructing a text through prediction and confirmation.

The next day, for ten minutes, the class wrote to 'show' from the perspective of one character what was going on in the story. Many identified with Matt and chose to write through his eyes and emotions. One very convincingly became a rather perceptive dog.

My owner had bin challenged to cross Deadman's Bridge, witch was just a fallen log over the brone-colored water of Deer Creek. It was just Yesterday, Friday. Hulk had announced to the class that my owner Matt was going to be the first to cross Deadmans Bridge. This announcement was a complete surprise to my owner, but there was nothing he could no now. Matts classmates knew he was afraid of the hazardous, brone-colored waters of Deer Creek. But now it was to late to turn back. Hulk who was big and strong and ruled with an iron hand. The bully was forcing Matt to do something he had put off far too long. Matt almost welcomed the bullys goading. I could tell he felled like a small fish in a big pond. "Hurry, chicken," commanded Hulk. He shoved Matt roughly. Matt's heart pounded and his face grew flushed as he glowered at thebully.
— Mike (11 years)

DRAFT

Extensions

1. With younger children, make the story artifacts more concrete. In a whole-group setting, the teacher presents, one by one, three or four artifacts of a character, encouraging the children to predict who might own these and what their life might be like. After this whole-group prediction, pairs of students are given one piece of paper with a photocopied picture from the story of the characters whose artifacts they saw. In pairs, children cluster their ideas, questions, and predictions about this character. After a whole-group sharing of their clusters, the story is read. The next day, children choose a way to demonstrate their understanding of the story.

2. Make character 'grab bags' of five or six artifacts for each group of four. Students cluster their ideas on one sheet of paper as to who this character might be and what his/her story is. After ten minutes of collaborative talk, students begin a ten-minute written account of their mystery character. Some of these are shared. The audience listens for artful use of the artifacts in the story and for examples of language which 'shows' rather than 'tells'. The next day, the 'grab bags' can be circulated to a new group of students.

3. Alternatively, make the 'grab bags' for each group of four students. Have the students talk about the contents of the bag, cluster for five minutes about their character, then move *as a group*, to a new character, leaving behind their character cluster. As the next group arrives 'at a new character', their task is to build on the existing idea cluster, integrating the previous group's cluster, the artifacts, and their own ideas. In this manner, the students move through all the bags, and back to their original character. After a review of the interpretations now available, they begin to write. This is also a good time for reflective writing, focused on the various interpretations of the artifacts (data).

4. This strategy works well in building understandings of people and cultures over time. Photographs, print materials, and souvenirs all make good building blocks.

BUILDING CHARACTERS: RECIPE

1. Choose 10-12 sentences or groups of sentences which focus on two characters to excerpt from a story. These can be direct speech, description, or narration.

2. Distribute these sentences to the students, one sheet per cooperative group of three students.

3. Instruct students to sort the sentences into two groups, one per character, and to use the information in these sentences to predict what they know about the two characters.

4. Allow about 15 minutes for the sorting and predicting.

5. Cluster this character information into two characters.

6. Compare how students have grouped the sentences by having them explain their reasoning and their evidence.

7. Individually, in their learning logs, have students reflect on what they noticed about their thinking and the connections they made in this part of the strategy.

8. Orally share predictions as to what will happen in the story.

9. Read the text.

10. Compare the author's version with the students' prediction.

5

Nurturing Poets

Using the *Nurturing Poets* strategy, we model moving from our own experience, through a selection of poems, to link to students' experiences and their poetic language, focusing on ideas, feelings, and images. The students collaborate to recognize effective communication in poetry and provide feedback to one another to enhance the development of powerful poems.

"The construction of new knowledge begins with our observations of events or objects through the concepts we already possess."

— Joseph D. Novak and D. Bob Gowin, *Learning How to Learn*.

"A memory that you choose to share, no matter how incidental, will almost certainly remind your listeners of some experiences of their own."

— S. Jeroski, D. Fisher, P. McIntosh, and H. Zwick, *Speak for Yourself*.

"Based on pre- and post-test measures and interview data, students engaged in writing remembered more of the poems' content, were more engaged in thinking about what they were reading, and were more sensitive to the author's craft. . . . Writing in the context of reading prompted deeper cognitive involvement in the task."

— William McGinley and Robert J. Tierney, "Reading and Writing As Ways of Knowing."

"Introducing children and poetry means being flexible and ready to experiment. . . . The introduction will be most effective if children have a part in selecting poems and devising ways by which they can hear the voice of the poet speaking to them personally."

— Nancy Larrick, "Keep a Poem in Your Pocket."

"It's our turn to decorate the front hall," my student teacher, Paula, reminded. "How about having the students write poetry to centre around Remembrance Day? But more a focus on peace. Could you show me what you'd do to get this kind of poetry?"

It was her immersion time and I hadn't taught the class for a couple of weeks. I didn't feel especially in touch with them, and being close to them always seemed important to me before doing a poetry lesson. It flashed through my mind how intuitively I teach such a lesson. How could I show her a planned way and in one lesson, hopefully, get the writing she had in mind? As an experienced teacher, I knew that when I hoped to lead the class to a particular theme I always accepted wherever their ideas took them. There could be a new meaning, a rare resemblance to my input! Still, I knew the serious yet relaxed attention I brought to the lesson was a key — and it held the intensity necessary to bring out real effort resulting in writing beyond a mere surface sing-song rhyme, writing that we felt had zing or heart. . . all the words we'd used to capture what good writing was.

We had looked at collections of poetry . . . the way it was all right to play and be imaginative and spontaneous in a humorous act. We also talked about how it was all right not to run away from direct looks at our own experience or emotions. When a student managed to carve just the right tension in a poem, to get the desired picture, we'd cheer. Though there must always be innumerable ways to state a thought, sometimes the writing we got was so clearly immediate and effective it seemed dressed in exactly the right and only possible words.

But how to deal with war and peace?

TEACHER: When I was young, boys and girls, I lived in Quebec near the Ottawa River. On hot summer days I'd look down from the hills where I picked beans at a market garden, and I'd watch the river far below. These were mostly scorching hot days with hardly any clouds, at least not until late afternoon when we got severe thunderstorms. . . .

Walking across the front of the room, I mused on a bit more about being a child myself. The children really listened, perhaps amazed that a teacher had once been young, too. Paula must have been wondering where all this was going.

TEACHER: I remember watching shapes in the few really fluffy clouds that appeared in exaggerated white against the blue, and wondering all sorts of things. Where our old dog was that was buried a few years before, what I'd be when I grew up, whether I'd be someone's mother someday. That thought seemed too amazing.

Only a couple of times had my father talked about war. He got a sick look on his face. He'd fought in Europe during World War II.

The teacher is making conscious an approach that has evolved for her over ten years.

In order to write poetry that is worth writing, students have to know and care about their subjects.

"Attention involves focusing energy, finding excitement in discovery — aha! and being very much awake." (McKim, 1980)

These were the words the children and I had generated in talking about writing that worked.

The clearer the image, the closer the fit of language to picture. When the students' inner picture was life-like, the writing had a realness to it.

The teacher is starting the process of wondering by modeling it from her own personal experience.

He never told stories or made it sound what it wasn't. I remember he said once he and another tail gunner were at the back of a plane that crashed one night in the mountains in Scotland. He said that the pilot and co-pilot didn't make it. He walked down the mountains in the morning. . . .

The class was attentive, focused.

TEACHER: What do you wonder about? Talk to a neighbor for a few minutes. What are some of your thoughts?

STUDENTS: I was telling Donnie about the break-in next door. I wonder if it'll happen to us next.

I wonder if I'll be rich and live in a mansion.

Sometimes I wonder about aliens. And black holes. Like if there are such things and if you'd get sucked in.

I do, too. And if there are other worlds. If the black hole is a tunnel to a different world.

About earthquakes, if B.C. is going to have one.

As students verbalize their thoughts, they actively engage with the topic. This sets the stage for further inquiry.

Several students nod wonderingly.

I jotted down a growing cluster of thoughts as the students spoke, inviting them to direct me where to connect their thoughts. They gave reasons and helped each other.

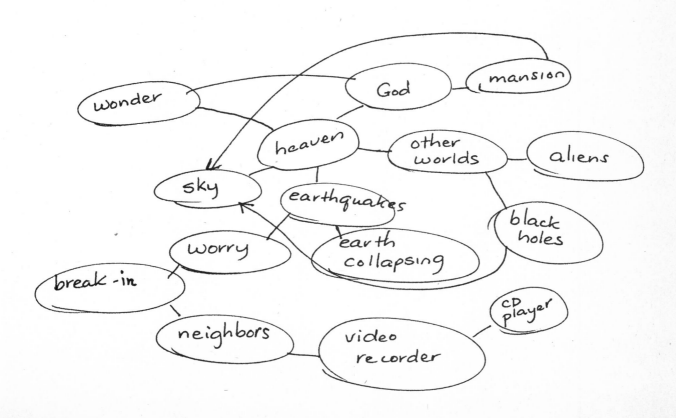

STUDENT: Mansions can go to sky, like a pie in the sky idea, you know, it probably won't come true. And black holes to sky. They're in it. Right? [laughter]

The cluster covered two boards by the time we stopped, yet it had taken just a couple of minutes. The students' answers reflected a lot of deep wondering and worry.

For the concept 'world' we clustered many ideas.

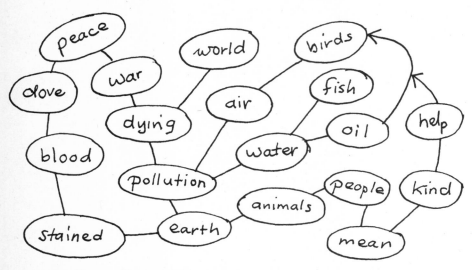

TEACHER: Remembrance Day is coming and we would like to put some of your writing around the school.

The teacher sets the purpose and audience for the writing.

Listen as I read what other poets have thought about war and peace and life, wondering the way we've been wondering together.

You may cluster in your notebooks words that strike you from the poems. Be aware of sounds and smells and touch senses along with the images the poet created.

The starting point of poetry is deep personal experience.

"In Flanders Fields" and other poems were read from the poetry anthology. Students noted ideas in various ways. Clustering was a routine practice for many. One sketched as I read. Another asked for the poems to be read one more time. A few closed their eyes, preferring to image this.

"Sensory experience that is not actively and consciously assimilated is also not readily remembered. (McKim, 1980)

Students represent their understandings in their preferred way. This allowing environment dignifies all learners.

TEACHER: As you read over the words, play with ideas, add from your own experiences, thoughts, wonderings, feelings — anything that crops up — happy, sad, confusing, whatever. Let's just see what happens. When you're ready, begin to draft freely, not worrying about whether it's going anywhere. Stay concentrated. We'll put the music on and write for 10 to 12 minutes. Then we'll see what we came up with. Any questions?

The music is part of sustaining the intensity of concentration. Slow classical music is a usual choice.

STUDENT: It's not just our minds. Remember that poem you read us.

TEACHER: Thanks. [A smile exchanged.]

How much they took in always amazed me. Not the whole class, but those who lapped language with a thirst that I, too, shared. After a silent reading period some weeks earlier, I'd read something Allen Ginsberg had said from the book I'd just been reading, something about poetry from a source deeper than the mind, "from the breathing and the belly and the lungs."

After daily silent reading the teacher frequently shares with the children passages that have been noteworthy.

Purpose filled the room. Kitaro music played softly as the writers engaged.

Some wrote within the general topic, others what came up as urgent or interesting to themselves alone. . . .

Paula and I also wrote, she from the back of the classroom, me from my place at the chalkboard. We stopped two to three minutes into writing, letting those with a strong need to hear their writing aloud, bounce it off the rest of us. I'd found these periodic stops important to sustaining the concentration. Also the extroverts seemed to die of internal pressure if they got a good line and couldn't share it quickly. The stops also helped those having trouble getting started by filling the air with possibilities, always accepted and warmly encouraged.

The teacher and any other adults in the room always model in the same process.

The break gives an immediate audience which helps the next part of the writing to develop.

Four students read the lines they'd written before the class bowed once again over pencils, etching their symbolic worlds into keytabs. "Never more truly alive," I thought to myself as they lost themselves again.

During the next break only one student wanted to share and only a few of the whole group even looked up. The class wrote for another twelve minutes.

TEACHER: Good, let's hear what happened.

STUDENTS: I wrote easily but I only liked one line.

I thought it was the wrong music for what I was trying to say.

It was great for a peace atmosphere. It sounds all spacey and calm.

TEACHER: Who would like to read part or all of a piece?

A literal sea of hands to go to the podium up front. No fear. Amazing ten- and eleven-year-old writers.

This was the crucial, sustaining point of my writing classes. The responses to a writer's attempt at self-expression had to be nurturing and disregarding all that didn't work. Only what worked was commented upon, and there was always a fresh look at something or a sound that was pleasing. The mega encouragement and no-risk context of these responding sessions released the timid, oh so self-conscious creative spirit of every student I ever had. Not to the same degree, but

The key to success is noticing what works. By making explicit fresh, alive language wherever it occurs, students begin to recognize effective writing. The response sessions nudge writing along.

always it did. By also commenting together on effective parts of published authors' writing as we did daily, whether in a reading lesson or from our ongoing novels read aloud, students, by being reflective in this way, had a continuous modeling. So the response time at the end of a writing class developed over the year. It was fortuitous to have part of the class for a second year as the new group of students could learn from the responses to another's writing. As well, they picked up the enthusiasm that was truly contagious.

Saturnin stood to read.

War Is a Video

Soldiers died and killed others for points.
The war went on and on.
The battlefield was like a graveyard.
The ground was sucking dead bodies' blood.
Blue flowers were starting to grow.
New generations became.
Big buildings started to grow.
In the depths of the land the blood is still there.

— Saturnin

STUDENTS: I like how you didn't have any extra words.

It is like a video how you wrote it, like your title.

I like how you said the ground sucked dead bodies' blood.

That part gave me an awful feeling but then you said blue flowers started to grow.

I liked how you said blue flowers, not just flowers.

TEACHER: I noticed you had a balance between the thought about war and then the life that followed. And then you had that line at the end that I thought was very effective — "In the depths of the land the blood is still there." It's as if you don't want us ever to forget. That picture stays with us in a haunting way. You really got something in this piece. . . .

Always specific comments, rather than "I like it", sometimes questions about how the student got or developed ideas.

PAULA: I know you came from Poland two years ago, Saturnin. Were you thinking about your country when you wrote that?

SATURININ: No, I wasn't.

STUDENT: You made it so real. Did you cluster first?

SATURININ: No. I try to see it. Then I write.

This was Saturnin's first year in a regular classroom situation. He had spent one year as an ESL student.

The teacher is continuously modeling or bringing to the conscious level what students hit upon naturally.

When teachers talk about metaphors and their effect in the work of authors they love, such imagery begins to appear in student work.

The charm and directness of this dark-haired boy — he feels good about the piece and our acknowledgment. I notice his self-esteem rise perceptibly.

TEACHER: Thank you, Saturnin. Would anyone else care to read? Carmen.

> War
>
> People fighting
> people killing others
> war is loved ones dying
> war is a bird that cannot fly.
>
> — Carmen

STUDENT: I like the end — ''a bird that cannot fly''. It's unusual.

TEACHER: It works in a way that's hard to state. What were you thinking of, Carmen?

CARMEN: It just came out like that. I don't really know how.

STUDENT: Maybe . . . all birds can fly, that's what birds do. War is so unnatural, it couldn't be right.

TEACHER: Thanks. Any other readers? Joe.

> Peace
>
> Nature all around
> The animals, the flowers, the birds
> Children climbing great big trees
> Most of all
> Peace is no wars
> Heaven is near.
>
> — Joe

TEACHER: I like the image of children climbing a big tree.

STUDENTS: ''Heaven is near'' is an effective ending, Joe.

I thought so too. It's soft.

TEACHER: In your learning logs I'd like you to reflect about your writing today.

Paula saw a lesson that went well, though lessons hadn't always been that smooth. This pattern or variations of it I'd used over the years with increasing ease. Some of our themes have included Christmas, love, spring, loneliness, and writing.

The teacher takes an active role in the same process as the class. This serious dialogue deepens the involvement in the craft.

The lesson ends with learners reflecting on their own processes.

Alone

Here I sit
Alone am I
Underneath the starlit sky
Where darkness is my only friend
And the night
sing its song of silence again
Forever in peace
and harmony
The swaying
from the trees
Here I sit
The night and I
Just beneath
the moonlit sky
I am forever alone

— Shani (12 years)

Love

As I was walking
through time
a bird sang
so wonderfully
I felt
as free as
a song in the wind
blowing
free of all fears
through time

— Chris (11 years)

Writing

Writing flows silently, like a ripple on a lake
It turns out beautifully, like swans when they wake
It comes from inside of you, and the right side of the brain
It may be either funny, sad, evil, or every really insane
When you write you're happy, or whatever it calls for
And all you want is to continue, all you want is more
It gives you a feeling of achievement, it gives you a sense of pride
If it comes from deep in you, you have nothing to hide
You may be writing seriously, you may do it just for fun
But once you've got the knack of it, your best has just begun.

— Patricia (12 years)

I'm going to make up a
pome it is calld Spring
Spring is here it's not the
wind it's not your
ammagganashon it's a
budding bloom a twingkd
in a happy eye a worrm
feeling rainbows in the
sprinkaller hot beachydays

A marragold smile in the
sun it's ballbss blooming
in the garden byootful

butterflys comeing out
of cocoons it's you
can almost here flowerssmileing

Melissa
(6 years)

48

NURTURING POETS: RECIPE

1. Teacher models by talking about her own experience with the topic.

2. Teacher reads examples from poetry anthologies.

3. Students cluster as teacher reads.

4. Class discusses ideas or feelings or images that struck them.

5. Students add to clusters, playing with ideas.

6. Students draft for approximately three to five minutes.

7. Teacher encourages them to share effective images.

8. Students continue drafting for an additional five to seven minutes.

9. Teacher suggests stopping to share, if students indicate desire.

10. Students finish drafting period — perhaps another three to five minutes.

11. Writers present from podium.

12. Both students and teachers respond to readings.

13. Students file their work in folders for possible publication (revise-edit-proofread-publish).

6

Reading Like an Expert

Building on the success of the *ReQuest* strategy, students work in small groups to predict, to generate and respond to 'in the text' and 'beyond the text' questions, to summarize, to clarify what has been read, and then to predict again. The active negotiation of understanding in *Reading Like an Expert* supports students becoming active, independent readers.

". . . researchers have found that emphasis on higher cognitive questions generally produces better learning than emphasis on fact questions . . . students also need to learn the response requirements of different types of questions . . . students were able to learn several question-answer relationships and use this knowledge to improve their reading comprehension."

— T.E. Raphael and J. McKinney, *An Examination of Fifth and Eighth Grade Children's Question-Answering Behavior: An Instructional Study in Metacognition.*

"Educators today know that the way a teacher structures a question influences the nature of the thinking required to respond. We also know that follow-up discussion strategies, such as asking for elaboration, influence the degree and quality of classroom discussion."

— Jay McTighe and Frank T. Lyman, Jr., *Cueing Thinking in the Classroom: The Promise of Theory-Embedded Tools.*

". . . critical literacy/thinking suggests the need for learners to do more with texts that simply soak up bits and pieces of information. It advocates the use of strategies and techniques for helping learners think critically."

— Marilyn Wilson, "Critical Literacy/Critical Thinking", in *Language Arts.*

"Allowing students to work in small groups gives them a greater share in the classroom's talk space. . . . The greater involvement . . . together with the greater opportunity to respond to and act on what others say make it a better situation for developing listening abilities."

— Jo-Anne Reid, Peter Forrestal, and Jonathan Cook, *Small Group Learning in the Classroom.*

TEACHER: This morning we are going to build on one of our favorite strategies, **ReQuest**. Sometimes we call it, *I'm the teacher, you're the teacher*. When I count to three, turn to the people in your group and tell them everything you know about the strategy. One, two, three.

The teacher walked slowly by the students, listening as they explained the details. These seven- and eight-year-olds were very comfortable with this process. After two or three minutes she invited the students to share their understandings.

The teacher is building on student knowledge of process.

TEACHER: As I point to your group, tell us one thing about **ReQuest**. We will continue around until we exhaust our ideas.

The students eagerly searched for details to add to the strategy's description. They had been working in these groups of three for a week now and I could see no reluctance to share ideas.

Student sharing serves as an assessment tool.

Some learning groups stay together for extended time periods.

TEACHER: ''You are right! Sometimes you will be the teacher and sometimes you will be the student. This time we are going to add more skills to **ReQuest**, skills that expert readers use. What is an expert?

Students are building on what they know.

STUDENTS: My Dad says he's getting an expert to come to look at our TV.

It's somebody who's good at things.

TEACHER: I wonder how you get to be an expert. Are any of you experts?

Melinda pointed to Jason. Jason beamed as Melinda explained that Jason was a lego master. Almost every day kids go to his house to build with lego. I decided that Jason's group would be my focus for this observation.

TEACHER: How did you get to be an expert with lego, Jason?

STUDENT: I do it all the time.

A story unfolded around Jason as he modeled many dimensions of expertise.

Students are creating their own concept of 'expert'.

TEACHER: Today we are going to read like experts. I wonder how an expert reads. What goes on inside an expert's head as he or she reads? Tell the people in your group what you think.

The students paused reflectively before offering ideas to each other. The teacher moved around the room noticing the interactions. She counted softly to five and the conversations stopped.

TEACHER: How does an expert read?

The teacher is connecting 'expert' to 'reader'

STUDENTS: They make pictures in their heads.

I think they tell someone about things.

Yes, my brother always tells me about his dinosaurs.

TEACHER: So you think experts do a lot of talking. I wonder what else experts do as they read? Tell your partners what you think about when you read.

The students searched to describe their own thinking. Students in my group told about books they were reading.

TEACHER: What did you learn from your partners?

STUDENT: When Christopher reads he gets right into the story.

Laughter erupted. Nods indicated many others saw themselves in the stories too.

STUDENTS: Sophia said when she reads she thinks about what is happening. She gets happy feelings. And she wonders about things.

Michael sneaks at night. He has a booklight and reads under the covers to find out about rocks.

Cathy is in the story.

TEACHER: Experts do all of those things. To read like experts today we'll predict what the story will be about by reading the title. Then we'll read one part together. I'll put the story on the overhead projector to make it easy for everyone to see.

The teacher is presenting a plan for practising expert behavior.

She flipped on the projector, held up four transparencies and explained the process about to unfold.

TEACHER: I've divided the story into four parts. After we have read each part, I will ask you a few questions. After we have talked about the questions, I'll be telling you what I think the first part was about. I'll tell you which words gave me some problems and what I think the next part of the story will be about. Then we'll change roles. You'll become the teachers and I will become the student.

The students recognized the familiar process. The teacher read the title, The Bear's Autumn, *and invited the students to predict in their learning logs, printing or drawing what they thought it would be about.*

TEACHER: Turn to your partners and share your predictions.

Sharing predictions hooks the students.

The teacher moved through the groups, noticing the many approaches to prediction. Some students were sketching; others were writing. Each student appeared comfortable with the sequence.

TEACHER: What did you notice about the ideas?

STUDENTS: They're all different.

   Some are the same too.

   I drew a tree and so did she.

TEACHER: Your ideas are very special to you. Every thinker makes his or her own ideas. As we read this morning, we'll learn about the author's ideas. What questions do you think we'll answer in the story?

Comprehending is a blend of text and experience.

STUDENTS: What happens to the bear?

   Maybe how he gets ready.

   About his house?

TEACHER: You seem like experts already. Just look at what you showed in your predictions and how you were able to ask such knowledgeable questions. Let's read the first part of the story. Who would like to be a teacher with me?

Smiles flashed and hands waved. She invited two complete groups (six children) to collaborate with her.

This increases opportunity for student talk with teacher scaffolding, as needed.

TEACHER: We will be asking you two kinds of questions. Sometimes you will be able to find the answers right in the story. At other times you will have to think beyond the story and bring in your own ideas.

She read the first passage. She asked the groups of students to think about the text and to try to anticipate what questions the teachers might ask. She gathered the group of six 'teachers' into a huddle and they developed two 'in the text' questions and two 'beyond the text' questions. She announced that the 'teachers' were ready and the students began the process.

The teacher is monitoring comprehension through active, ongoing questioning.

Students also think like active readers.

STUDENT TEACHER: This one you can find in the story. What was the name of the bird?

The teacher scanned the class. Since he asked the question, he got to choose the person to answer.

Teacher alerts responders to appropriate reading behavior in their answer search.

STUDENT: A jay.

The teacher thanked the student and another student teacher asked a question.

STUDENT TEACHER: This answer isn't in the story. What do you think the bears were eating?

Four hands waved confidently.

STUDENT: Berries.

The teacher moved to the side of the room. She spoke when an opportunity arose to have the students elaborate or substantiate their thinking.

TEACHER: What made you say ''berries''?

STUDENT: I know about bears. My Mom and I got a book at the library. It tells all about bears.

Teacher encourages articulation of child's experience to enhance transfer of the thinking involved.

TEACHER: My, it's lucky for us that we have a bear expert to help us today. Thank you.

The student teachers asked two more questions before moving into summarizing.

TEACHER: Let's look at the passage and see if we can tell you what it was about. Students, turn to your partners and talk together. We'll share our thoughts in two or three minutes.

The teacher group huddled again to talk about the text. The students talked, referring many times to the text.

TEACHER: What was that part about?

The teacher invited her student teacher colleagues to respond. Their collaborative talk had helped them to define the big picture.

STUDENT TEACHERS: A bear family getting ready for winter.

It's about when the leaves fall and the bears sleep.

Summarizing reconstructs the big ideas as experienced by the students.

TEACHER: Would any of you like to add any details.

STUDENT: It's not about here. It's in Japan.

TEACHER: Teachers, do you see any words or ideas that you wonder about?

Specific vocabulary knowledge enhances comprehension.

All of the students scanned the text. One student teacher raised her hand.

STUDENT TEACHER: I wonder what ''aflame'' means.

TEACHER: How could we figure that out?

STUDENT: I think it's like a forest fire.

TEACHER: Let's read it again.

The teacher read the sentence. You could see the students connecting with the vocabulary, using the context to unlock the meaning.

Teacher models a strategy for developing vocabulary.

TEACHER: Don't you get that satisfied feeling when something makes sense? I know I do. Our last job, as teachers, is to predict what will happen next. You predict with your group, while we think together.

The small groups buzzed with ideas while the teachers conferred.

After a few minutes they shared their predictions. People in the student group offered further possibilities.

TEACHER: What do you think happens next?

The students reminded her that it was their turn to be the teachers. The teacher group returned to their places with a round of applause acknowledging their contribution. The teacher put the second piece of text on the projector. This time they read it silently. All of the students became teachers and created questions.

As they talked, they had no difficulty thinking up questions. The teacher invited a group of six volunteers to join her in the role of students answering the questions. The teacher moved in and out of the role of 'student' when she focused the teacher groups on summarizing and clarifying. Everyone wrote predictions in their logs. The class processed the four pieces of text, experiencing the 'teacher' role and the 'student' role twice.

With guided practice, students generate a variety of question types with ease.

TEACHER: We worked as expert readers today. Turn to your partners and share what you noticed about your learning.

Not at all to my surprise, the students loved the teacher role.

Extensions

1. The next day, to deepen the connections, the teacher read the students an image sequence from the story. After interviewing the students in role, she developed a 'talk show' by having students think like the characters and respond in role. The students clamored for the interview chairs. Their character elaborations demonstrated perceptive understanding.

2. Alternatively, the students can draft to retell the story. To activate memory, they recall the sequence in four pictures and then write.

Once a Boot a time

then Was a shadow
in the Buches it
Was some Bears. They
Were geting ready
to hibrnat. They were eating
Wild Berry Grapes. Baby bear
clamed a tree and
saw wonderfd Montuns,
and a beautiful pond.
He seen some
Silver samon.

Jesse

3. Older students often use a response form to record their developing comprehension. These drafts provide rich data for the documentation of growth and make visible the links between content and process.

Response Draft

Strategy: Reading Like an Expert

Student's Name: _Rueben_   Date/s: _____

Thinking About Experts

stop to think   look for infrmtion
make pictures

Predictions

uncomfortble sleeping on the floor and hard to get food because it is in the winter. It would be cold in the morning because there would be no fire. It would be stuffy in the long house because of smoke from the fire.

Questions Before We Read

Would you have furs on to go out to play?

In the Text	Moving Beyond the Text
Question(s)	
What kind of chores would you have? Why did they scrub with cedar?	How dose bathing in ice water and scrubbing make you strong? Would you feel lonely?

Summary

It was about the Indian children's jobs and how they had to work to please their family.

Things I Wonder About

Would you get free time?

Predictions

We think the next part is going to be about the elders and what they do to help the tribe.

READING LIKE AN EXPERT: RECIPE

1. The teacher groups the students, three to five per group.

2. The teacher establishes the plan for reciprocal teaching.

3. Students write or recall how experts read.

4. Individually, students write or sketch predictions.

5. Students share predictions with partners.

6. Students generate questions and offer hypotheses before reading.

7. A group of students joins the teacher and collaboratively creates 'in the text' and 'beyond the text' questions. The other students talk to anticipate questions the 'teachers' might ask.

8. The 'teacher' group collaboratively models summarizing and clarifying. Each time this group huddles to confer, the others talk to anticipate.

9. 'Teachers' return to their places to predict.

10. Students become 'teachers' at their places. They collaborate to create questions.

11. A group of students joins the teacher to field the questions.

12. The 'teachers' collaborate to summarize and clarify.

13. Both groups write to predict.

14. The teacher repeats the process with more sections of text.

15. Students reflect on what they did and why.

7

Listen — Sketch — Draft

The *Listen-Sketch-Draft* strategy encourages students to sketch their thoughts while listening, to talk to a partner about their sketches, to talk about their thinking and the 'big ideas' of the passage, and then to draft a summary using those 'big ideas'. During a typical sequence, students would listen, sketch, and draft three times and reflect on the process. Criteria for powerful summaries is developed with the students.

"... children use drawing as a language for processing information, formulating ideas, articulating emotions, and communicating with others. Drawing, therefore, plays an important role in the intellectual, emotional, and social development of children."

— Bob Steele, *Drawing Network Newsletter.*

"Unhesitating sketching response to each idea that arises creates a momentum in which expression keeps pace with thinking. . . . Idea sketches are a remarkable extension of imagination, a kind of visible graphic memory."

— Robert H. McKim, *Thinking Visually.*

"I have a simple test of teacher evaluation expertise which can be used as a self-test. Look at the impromptu description of a particular child's literacy development. Two features most evident in an expert's description will be an emphasis on processes and an emphasis on what the child can do."

— Peter Johnston, *Teachers as Evaluation Experts.*

"Collegial practice expands cognitive complexity, leads to thoughtful planning, and increases teacher's satisfaction with their work."

— Linda Lambert, *The End of an Era of Staff Development.*

TEACHER: What are you noticing about your thinking as you see so many teachers with us today? Turn to your partner and share your thoughts.

Slight apprehension filled this early intermediate class as they prepared to engage in a demonstration. Their classroom teacher and a district consultant were about to teach a one-and-a-half hour sequence, side-by-side with ten teachers observing. This was the first in a cycle of four staff development sessions. Each session included staff planning, observing students in process, reflecting, and further planning.

TEACHER: Are you wondering why the other teachers are here? Any ideas?

The students glanced around shrugging their shoulders. They seemed to be searching for possible clues.

STUDENTS: To watch us work?

To tell our brothers and sisters about us.

TEACHER: We are working together on ways to make learning better for you. As we work together on a new strategy this morning, you will really be teaching us what works and how we can make it better. The teachers will be noticing what you can do and how you think. After recess we will share what we noticed and plan another set of strategies to try with another class.

The students relaxed, whispering to their partners. They had been grouped in twos with each staff member observing one pair of students.

TEACHER: In this strategy sequence you will listen and sketch as we continue to read about the Gold Rush in your social studies text. Both of us will take turns leading the class. You will need to experiment to see how you prefer to sketch. Some people like to sketch as they listen. Others like to hear the whole passage before beginning. We will give you about three minutes to work on your sketches after we read. Then we will talk about your sketches and think about the big ideas in the passage. You will write what the passage was about in the numbered boxes. Ask me questions about the process.

STUDENT: Do we use the whole space to sketch?

TEACHER: That's up to you. We will be reading three passages. Some people will sketch each passage separately. Others will sketch a whole picture incorporating the ideas. Once you have experienced the strategy, you will know more about what works best for you. Be sure to notice your thinking as we move through the different steps.

In demonstration lessons, the teacher begins by acknowledging the viewers and their role in the class.

Focusing an observation on just two students gives time for scripting the language of the children and seeing the lesson through two children's eyes. Later, teachers refine the instruction based on authentic learner response.

An overview of the lesson is presented and student expectations clarified. Students are reminded of opportunities for choice in sketching.

Does everyone have a response sheet? Good. Let's begin.

When you listen to stories, tapes, people talking, what do you notice about your thinking? In the first space on your response sheet, jot down a few ideas.

The teacher links other student listening experience to today's task.

After two or three minutes of writing, the students shared their thinking with their partners, noticing the ways they represented their ideas. The teacher established a rhythmic clap as a signal to complete the talking.

*This is an adaptation of **Think-Pair-Share** (Kagan, 1989).*

TEACHER: When you are listening, what do your thoughts look like?

STUDENTS: I feel my brain moves as I study the words.

Cranking. It's like the gears that move together. I can feel the puzzle pieces fall into place.

The voice comes through my ears. I think of other ideas. It makes me wonder why they think that way.

I feel the blood travel fast when I think. Some parts of my brain start to thump.

With math I actually see equations and I try to move things around to figure it out.

Searching. I wonder how the person thought of it. I see lots of pictures and sometimes I feel the temperature.

*This was the second lesson on the Gold Rush. Yesterday the students had begun with a familiar strategy, **I Know, I Wonder** (Palinscar, et al, 1985).*

Unit planning involves a sequence of strategies.

TEACHER: Let's begin. I'll read. You listen and decide how to approach the sketching.

The teacher read the first few paragraphs. Most of the students listened, holding back on the drawing. Both of the students I was observing began sketching immediately. One stopped after a few seconds and a puzzled look crossed her face. She put her pencil down and waited until the end of the passage to continue. After the three minutes the teacher invited the partners to talk about their drawings, and then to share their ideas with the class.

TEACHER: I noticed one student start sketching and then stop. Can you tell us about that?

The teacher had moved over beside the student's desk. A shy smile reflected pleasure in being noticed.

STUDENT: I had trouble listening and sketching at the same time. I couldn't seem to keep up with the ideas. So I decided to wait. I tried to listen and make pictures in my head first.

The teacher supports different approaches to learning.

A few nods acknowledged similar experiences.

TEACHER: What were other people's experiences?

STUDENT: The drawing helped me out a lot. I noticed it was easier after I got going. I got a few ideas from my partner. Our drawings were so different, even though we had almost the same ideas.

TEACHER: Your thinking shows such detailed understanding. Now look at your drawings and talk about the big ideas in the passage. When you are ready, write your version in box one on your sheet.

Student talk prior to writing offers wider possibilities.

The students reflected together, recreating the essence of the text's meaning. Each moved easily into the writing. The teacher moved around the room, noticing and encouraging. She invited responses from each set of students.

TEACHER: Let's hear your big ideas. Hold the passage in your mind as you listen and notice if the words capture the big ideas.

STUDENTS: James Douglas delivering gold to the mint on a boat called ''The Otter''.

''The Otter'' sailing off with a shipment of gold in February.

It was about securing the gold for the journey to the San Francisco mint.

This part was about ''The Otter'' carrying the gold to San Francisco for the Hudson Bay Company.

In 1858 a ship called ''The Otter'' carried gold as the cargo from the gold rush with James Yale on board writing his diary.

TEACHER: What did you notice?

STUDENTS: They mostly had the same idea but they said it in different ways.

Not too many words. I went right back into the story.

TEACHER: How will you approach the sketching this time?

Two-thirds of the class raised their hands. The experience with the process gave them new understandings to draw upon.

The focus is on the representation of thinking, not the quality of the drawing.

TEACHER: Try to capture as many aspects of the thoughts as you can.

She read a longer passage covering five paragraphs. Many students experimented with the sketching as the text was being read. Others listened intently. Everyone was intensely involved in representing their ideas. I was amazed at how much I was able to notice about the two students I was observing. The teacher spoke softly to move the students into talk.

TEACHER: Talk about the big ideas and summarize your ideas in the second box. If you find you have time, write in the box something you wonder about.

Questions begin to surface as new information is added.

Many of the students moved into the writing naturally.

TEACHER: As we hear the summaries this time, listen for powerful ways the writers have used to put their ideas together.

They begin to develop criteria for summarization.

STUDENT: Thompson River had gold and everyone heard about it.

TEACHER: What struck you?

STUDENTS: I liked the power in his voice.

He got the whole idea.

TEACHER: Let's hear another summary.

STUDENT: This part was about the person that found a shiny pebble, took it to trade and got many furs in return.

The teachers and students processed three passages, sketching, summarizing and developing criteria. By the end of the sequence they had a beginning list to build from:

A Summary

- accurate information
- word choice that holds the whole idea
- gets to the point
- captures the feeling
- the way it is read can really add meaning

TEACHER: We have worked hard this morning expressing our ideas in many ways. Talk to your partner about what we did and why we did it. Then write what you noticed about your thinking in the last box on your response sheet.

Reflection deepens student understanding of process.

STUDENT: You might think you can't, but if you think you can think you think better.

Many giggles erupted from this tongue-twister.

STUDENTS: I noticed that I had more trouble drawing the pictures when the reading was longer.

Gradually it got easier.

I was thinking a lot. I was thinking so much that I was tired. . . . In other words, half-dead.

When I was drawing I was able to think better about what I was going to write.

I noticed that my mind learned more about the gold rush. It was easy to reassemble the stuff.

I noticed that I thought harder than I ever thought before.

The teaching team reflected on what they had learned from the process. The students seemed glued to each spoken word.

The class is a community of learners.

TEACHER: Thank you for sharing your learning with us today. We are going to move into the library to share what we have learned.

The teachers gave the students a round of applause before leaving.

The teacher observed that Troy "showed thinking in bubbles." Also, he "made a list in the first two boxes and was able to write a one-statement summary and a question in the third box."

The boat from the Hudson Bay company with the gold.

1

an Indian finding gold where the Jonsson and the Fraser river meet.

2

The man from the mint telling all the other men that the next gold rush would be at the Thompson and Fraser river.

3

What I noticed about my thinking

When I was drawing I was able to think better about what I was going to write.
—Alice

The teacher observed that Alice "used thinking bubble's after Troy's suggestion." Also, "each passage led to more expanded expression."

Teacher Observation Form

Strategy: Listen—Sketch—Draft

Date:_____

Student	Interaction • with partner • with whole class	Sketching	Summarizing	Reflections
Troy	• animated once he began explaining his picture • listened to partner and built on her ideas. • asked questions • elaborated to class when invited to	• started out with tiny drawings • after first passage drew whole picture • showed thinking in bubbles • detail expanded with each reflection	• made a list in first two boxes • able to write a one-statement summary and a question	• statement • "Gradually it got easier."
Alice	• hesitant to share drawing. Said, "Mine's not very good." • after sharing, tried partner's idea • volunteered when teacher asked	• erased, visibly uneasy about sketch • used thinking bubbles after Troy's suggestion	• a fact, not a full statement • each passage led to more expanded expression	• "When I was drawing I was able to think better about what I was 'going to write'."

Comments: Both hesitated initially, but the sketching seemed to pull them in. The initial reluctance disappeared.

Extension 1

The teachers began their dialogue on the demonstration sequence by sharing what they had noticed about the students they had been observing.

The two teachers leading the demonstration shared details of their planning and reflected on what they had noticed. The teachers then formed pairs and moved into five groups each with a different colored felt pen. On a large piece of paper they reflected on the details of the strategy, listing all of the attributes. They also listed questions. After ten minutes the papers rotated. Each pair read the new paper, added details, answered questions, and added new connections. The papers rotated three times before each pair summarized what they now knew about the strategy. Questions and answers led to the planning of how the staff members would use this strategy in different areas of the curriculum. The teachers planned to do the strategy alone, or side-by-side as it had been modeled, three times before the next session in three weeks.

The teachers reflected in their response logs on this approach to staff development:

"If we are going to teach children to be thinkers and writers, teachers need to go through the processes. Talking about the strategies really helps to connect all of our good ideas."

"The strategies were more visible when you observed in the classroom. It reinforced and extended my understandings and helped me to realize that learning occurs in the most powerful situations — thinking situations."

"I felt more comfortable being in my own school with kids I knew. I could really see the effect."

Extension 2

In one Grade 1 class the students summarized through pictures.

Primary **Thinking Paper** *by Sherine (5 years)*

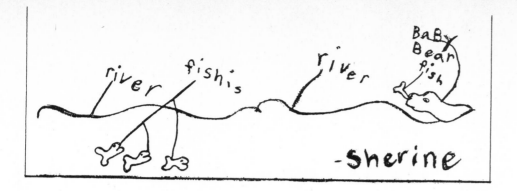

Extension 3

Fiona Morrison, a primary consultant in Langley, used **Listen-Sketch-Draft** as a buddy activity with four- and five-year-olds. They listened, talked, and sketched together. She had one group of buddies retell the story to another pair of buddies.

Primary **Thinking Paper** *by Allison (5 years) and Alicia (4 years).*

Extension 4

Choose a challenging passage, rich in concepts. Each student works from one piece of paper divided into four quadrants. Label the quadrants *emotions, talk, pictures,* and *senses.* As the teacher reads and rereads the passage, students cluster and sketch to represent their understanding in and among the quadrants. After sharing with a partner and the whole class, students summarize what they have learned.

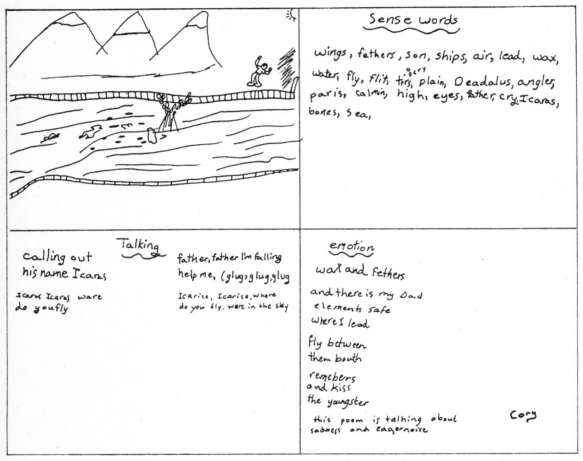

Thinking Paper by *Cory*
(*11 years*).

The Time of Hardships

. . . a nearby dog breaks the silence. The memory of Icrus pains Daedalus so. Every time Daedalus thought of Icarus a big sore in his heart wells up, into a ball. This is a special but painful day. Daedalus had to bury his son's treasures along with his memories. The minutes passed like seconds and hours passed like minutes. The time to bury Icarus and all hope and happiness. . . . Daedalus moped outside and saw Icarus float to the heavens. The tears of joy roll down. The sore has healed.

Cory (11 years)

LISTEN — SKETCH — DRAFT: RECIPE

1. Students write or sketch, recalling their thinking during a listening experience.

2. Students share their ideas with partners, then with the whole class.

3. Students fold a response sheet into six boxes or set up a page in their learning logs.

4. Students listen to a passage, choosing to sketch as the teacher reads or after the teacher reads.

5. Students share approaches.

6. Students talk about the 'big ideas' in the passage.

7. Individually, they write a summary.

8. Students listen to drafts to establish criteria for powerful summaries.

9. Teacher processes two more passages.

10. Students reflect on their thinking in the last box, share with partners and then with the whole class.

8

Drama into Persuasive Writing

The use of *Role Drama* as a learning tool enables students to live the experience prior to writing about it. This 'hands-on' experience of using *Drama into Persuasive Writing* builds belief, commitment, and understanding of new knowledge in a natural way. Newly learned concepts are easily remembered and built upon in subsequent lessons.

"When the students 'become' someone else and enter the fictional 'here and now', they have the opportunity to work inside a story, connecting their own emotions, experiences, and values with the situations and themes of literature. This is drama."

— Larry Swartz, *Dramathemes*.

"For classroom drama to succeed, both teacher and children will have to create a supportive social climate in which children are encouraged to express their ideas freely, to respect each other's opinions, and to accept group decision."

— Patrick Verriour, "Drama in the Whole-Language Classroom," in *Whole-Language Practice and Theory*, Victor Frose, editor.

"Talk is one of the most important media of personal creativity. Perceptive and challenging discussion strengthens the intellect and provides for the best transfer of under-standings and thinking skills across the curriculum."

— Joan Dalton, *Adventures in Thinking*.

"Through talk children negotiate not only their own learn-ing but also their place in the classroom world and beyond. Accordingly, all children must be given opportunities to develop the ability to talk in a variety of settings."

— Barry Dwyer, *A Sea of Talk*.

TEACHER: What I'd like to do today is some role drama.

The Grade 5/6 class murmured. They were both worried and excited about this new venture.

TEACHER: It's not like acting, like people doing different roles in a theatre. It's more like becoming someone else, and talking and thinking the way you think that person would. Because you are interested in animals, I thought I'd read you some of my favorite animal poems.

The students leaned towards her. She read verses from Ogden Nash, funny and full of good sounds.

The poetry reading sets the stage for identifying with the animals and establishing a commitment to the problem.

TEACHER: Well, that poem reminds me of a book, *The Day the Zoo Went on Strike.* Have you ever heard of that?

STUDENTS: No.

TEACHER: Well, not many people have.

She started retelling the story, using voices — words spoken by the animals in the tale. The animals were discussing among themselves their views of living in confinement in a zoo. After some disgruntled talk, a decision was arrived at to go on strike the next day. Strike day found no movement in any of the cages. At closing time, coming to life, the animals discussed their perception of people's behavior. They decided that people were a lot like zoo animals. Maybe the one-day strike was enough. And so it was that the strike got called off.

Through story retelling, she models the characters' voices and action.

Meanwhile, talk was around in the community about unusual goings-on in the zoo. People returned the next day with quite different behaviors. They looked and saw the animals just as they were. They clapped and appreciated them.

TEACHER: And that's the story I heard.

The children in the silent room wanted to go back into the story. The teacher had woven an inviting place.

Just enough details have been woven to encourage students to want to read the story independently.

TEACHER: I was reading about zoo animals and found out that a quarter of all deaths result from animals eating items given to them by zoo visitors.

The teacher makes references to varied reasons why readers read.

Distressed looks matched her serious news.

TEACHER: Arranging a zoo must be a lot of work and requires careful planning as to where to put it and where to arrange all the things that need to go into it once it's got a location.

Movement from fantasy to fiction to fact helps build belief.

STUDENTS: Yes.

> I knew a zoo keeper once. He had a really important job.

> I know someone who designs aquariums.

TEACHER: I thought we'd do a drama about people who are arranging a zoo, people who've been given thirty acres and don't have much money. What animals might we have in our zoo?

STUDENTS: Tigers.

> Cheetahs.

> Monkeys and zebras.

> Llamas.

> Fish.

> Werewolves.

TEACHER: Are they mythic? We'll have to investigate that.

STUDENTS: Timber wolves.

> Elephants.

> Snakes.

> Skunks.

> Falcons.

TEACHER: We're at a convention, so you'll each need a name, a serious, grown-up name — Professor Brunswick, Mrs. Caldwell, Mrs. Renwick. . . . Good, using nametags, print yours and pin it on.

Names reinforce the mantle of the expert and maintain belief.

The students worked quickly and sat in groups of four, ready, nametags visible.

TEACHER: A good way to start a drama is to close your eyes and leave all other thoughts behind.

Ladies and gentlemen, thank you for answering my call. You are all experts on various animals.

Teacher in role sets the tone of seriousness.

In groups of four, I'd like you to come up with an animal you would like us to fund. Your group will have to decide what animal. After coming to group consensus on your animal, send one representative to the architect's office for supplies for your group's requirements. Discuss the environment necessary for your animal and any special features you'd like our zoo to include. There are resource materials around the convention room. Some of you may have written some yourselves. Feel free to use what is there.

Collaboration with librarian has made available much print material.

The students dispersed to find information, pooled the books they'd found, and began to read. The room was mostly quiet, with some whispers and recording of facts. The information search was purposeful. Students had selected their own animal and once they knew what environment was required, they used the information to create an appropriate zoo environment, 'as experts'. The students in role played seriously and well. Little silliness was noted, the teacher's composure in the room lending an authority to the activity. Information started to be recorded on chart paper. Special features included amenities for people.

The recess bell interrupted. After an hour into the lesson, the students filed out still chattering about conditions for their animals. As they returned to the room, the teacher met them in role.

The students were reading as purposeful experts searching for information which they could use.

TEACHER: Ladies and gentlemen, a reminder that to come back into the drama, you should close your eyes, leave behind who you are, and once again become the expert.

Teacher requests immediate re-entry into role.

The student groups moved to work areas again. They were barely settled in when a raised, anxious voice (the teacher) pounded.

TEACHER: Sorry to disturb you. Can you come to a big meeting right away? It's an emergency! Our plans are being challenged. A development group has said zoos are of no value to society. They are planning to develop this land for houses. Are zoos important?

STUDENTS: Yes.

TEACHER: Why do you think they are?

STUDENTS: For families and fun.

> Fresh air.

> To do things together.

> To save the animals.

> We could strike, builders can't cross picket lines.

> Don't we already own the land?

TEACHER: The city council will make the final decision about how the land will be used. The developers say the animals are happy where they are; they shouldn't be put in zoos. What do you say?

STUDENTS: Oil spills are killing all kinds of wildlife, especially birds and otters.

> Bald eagles are dying.

> I saw on TV that drift nets are killing everything — like porpoises and everything. They drown.

Animals in Africa are being killed for furs and tusks and
the meat is left to rot.

TEACHER: There are some developers who would like to come to
the meeting. They think families need houses.

*Six students volunteered to be developers and arrived to debate the
issue.*

TEACHER: Talk in small groups about how to plan your arguments.

*The groups huddled and talked animatedly for five minutes. The six
developers sat on chairs arranged to face the group.*

TEACHER: As you know, ladies and gentlemen, this meeting has
been called because a lot of us have put a lot of energy into
planning a zoo and a new group has come forward to say they
want the land. Mrs. Caldwell, would you introduce your committee?

The developers stood ceremoniously.

STUDENT (AS MRS. CALDWELL): I understand you'd like a zoo. But
more and more families are coming from Asia and they
need houses.

TEACHER: Anyone like to address the question?

STUDENT (AS MR. ENGERTIGER): Animals are becoming extinct —
people are not.

TEACHER: This report may go out to the newspapers. Do we want
to appear as not caring about people?

STUDENT (DEVELOPERS): We agreed that we are on a short budget. If
you were a person immigrating to Canada, you would
expect a house. They'll have to be on the street.

STUDENT (ZOO): You could find more land somewhere else. There
are big trees, too, on this land.

STUDENT (DEVELOPERS): That's the land our fund suppliers want.

STUDENT (ZOO): Why don't we have half the land and you have
half?

STUDENT (DEVELOPERS): Well, I'll ask my rich friends if they'll go for
half the land.

TEACHER: We must also remember that the council must pass the
decision. It's up to them.

I can see there is a lot of discussion here. I know you have many
excellent ideas carefully thought out why people need a zoo as well

*Genuine language use is
provided by teacher in role.*

as you who are the developers, why you need the land. Those ideas need to be carried to the public. The public needs both sides of the issue. I'd like you to begin to get your message out in a newsletter.

Individually students quickly got down to writing. They have written every day since school opened a few weeks ago. As they finished writing they drifted towards the architect's office where they continued to work on the zoo planning model.

TEACHER: Now that you have a draft of your ideas, let's come together.

The students moved to the sharing area and read several of their drafts.

Dear Editor:
    I am a land developer. My company is Reid Houses. I am depending on getting the thirty acres. I think animals are getting better treatment than people. Besides there are enough zoos in this country. I hope I get the thirty acres to build houses on.

                                              Yours truly,
                                              Bob Reid

Dear Editor:
    I am part of the Tiger Lily Zoo Company. There are many animals that are so cute and they don't deserve to be deserted. Animals need to be free. But there are many dangers in the world, and animals are part of them.
    Poachers are killing endangered species. Zoos are helpful to the animals of our world. They help with grooming and health needs too.
    Zoos help families be together on Sundays. Please help. That's all we ask.

                                              Yours truly,
                                              Tiger Lily Zoo Company

TEACHER: This gentleman has some important ideas to put forth. He hasn't decided which side he's on yet. He suggests we make it a park — a third possibility. He told me that privately. At the moment he is not giving his ideas to the press.

Teacher focuses on recognition of the diversity of individuals, honoring all.

She had masterfully included the 'reluctant speaker'. She drew the two-and-a-half hours to a close, saying that ultimately the decision rested with council, that the letters would tell members rather well what opinions the two sides had put forth. She told the delegates she had been impressed with the serious tone of their letters as well as the arguments.

That day their learning logs reflected their reactions to the role-playing approach:

I enjoyed pretending to be a different person. I especially liked being a land developer and expressing my feelings.

Christina (10 years)

I liked drawing the zoo plans. It was fun working with other people.

Trent (11 years)

I like doing that because I like debates and I like to pretend stuff like that. I liked acting like an adult and feeling like I was an author and a very important person.

Becky (11 years)

I liked wearing a nametag.

Chad (10 years)

The lesson had been most engaging for the students. Their full attention was given throughout. They listened in silence to readings and storytelling; they spoke out in the large group and with their smaller groups; they read for information, collaborated, and wrote easily. Their logs, the first entries they had made, spoke of enjoyment. I was pleased with the sensible arguments they had made in their first attempts at persuasive writing.

DRAMA INTO PERSUASIVE WRITING: RECIPE

1. Students choose a topic they wish to explore deeply.

2. Teacher sets the context for learning by viewing, reading and storytelling from a variety of text and media.

3. Teacher introduces the issue and develops the setting for the drama.

4. Students, in role, name themselves.

5. They begin role drama with an image.

6. Students work, in role, on their assigned tasks, collecting information.

7. Teacher, in role, checks on understandings and beliefs being established.

8. In small groups, students prepare for the debate.

9. Students debate, in role.

10. Students write to persuade, using the understandings and beliefs they have developed in role.

11. Students file their letters in their writing portfolios for possible revision once time has passed, thought has changed, and interest allows.

9

The Language of Pictures

Using story clips, or images, to create a shared framework, students work with partners to view a picture from the text and recreate this picture in words for others who are recreating it, unseen, as a sketch. Sketchers ask clarifying questions based on what they need to know. The *Language of Pictures* strategy has students experience each role of describer and sketcher twice. Students really reach for language to express their thinking with this strategy.

"Split images promotes careful observation, clarity of expression, and listening. Piecing together what is heard and what is seen develops skill in sequencing and a sense of story. Interpreting the partial information seen and heard requires numerous inferences."

— Terry D. Johnson and Daphne R. Louis, *Bringing It All Together*.

"Listening is a combination of hearing what another person says and a suspenseful waiting, an intense psychological involvement with a person talking."

— R. Bolton, *People Skills*.

"A search for precise verbal description does three things: (1) it enhances visual memory by relating visual imagery to existing verbal knowledge, (2) it disciplines seeing by joining verbal and visual searching together, and (3) it educates ambidextrous thinking."

— Robert H. McKim, *Thinking Visually*.

". . . children use drawing as a language for processing information, formulating ideas, articulating emotions, and communicating with others. Drawing, therefore, plays an important role in the intellectual, emotional, and social development of children."

— Bob Steele, *Drawing Network Newsletter*.

TEACHER: You have just heard five story clips from *The Dragon Nanny* to give shape to your predictions. Turn to your partner and share how you think the story will unfold. I will clap in two or three minutes to signal that you have 30 seconds to finish your conversation.

The students were sitting in two large groups, each group facing the other. They had written their individual predictions about the story after the teacher had read the excerpts.

TEACHER: You certainly were involved in sharing your predictions quickly. Who would like to share with the whole class?

STUDENTS: I think this story will be about two baby dragons lost somewhere. They get trapped in this contraption and get taken hostage by some men that live in a castle. They will catch the dragons and keep them so that they don't scare the townspeople anymore.

I think the story is about six baby dragons and they all split apart and are killed in a sand pit. They will never be found for millions and millions of years.

Several predictions were shared, students giving a variety of story possibilities based on the clips they had heard.

TEACHER: What did you notice about your thinking as you listened to the predictions?

STUDENTS: I could see my story lined up beside each prediction.

I put myself in Nanny's place.

I was making pictures in my mind about what would happen next, and what is happening. I was sort of brainstorming.

TEACHER: Lots of different things were going on in your minds. Now we are going to use the **Language of Pictures** strategy to learn more about the story.

The students buzzed with excitement. This strategy had obviously been anticipated by the seating arrangement.

TEACHER: Who can review for us the process of this strategy?

STUDENTS: Half the class gets a picture and the other half gets paper to sketch on. The ones with the picture try to tell the others about the picture so they can draw it. And the drawers get to ask questions.

Story impressions offered prior to reading prompt engagement with the text.

The 30 seconds acknowledges the need to draw your conversation to a close.

This management comment reflects their task commitment.

Elements from the story clips are woven into the predictions.

A context for, and expectation of, reflection are established. Externalizing thoughts helps make new connections.

Students reconstruct their understanding of the strategy.

You don't have to sketch. You can just listen.

We try and help the drawers make this picture on the screen inside their heads.

Students who are not yet ready are not forced into the physical drawing of a sketch, but they can practise mentally.

TEACHER: While you are describing and listening, you may want to think about the parts of a thought which help us remember. Can you help me fill in my four circles?

With input from the students, the teacher filled in the circles and connected them with lines. I recognized the students' personalization of Marzano's (1986) thought components.

The teacher invites students to move beyond a literal retelling of the picture.

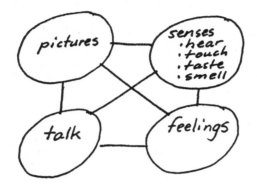

She handed out a copy of the text, open to the same picture, to each pair of students on the viewing side, and a blank sheet of paper to each student on the sketching side.

Formulating hypotheses sets a purpose for listening.

TEACHER: Sketchers, please write down a couple of questions that you have about the story before we begin. If you choose, you may talk to your partner for ideas before you begin. While they are talking, describers may talk with their partners for two or three minutes to plan the information you will share.

As the students talked, the teacher listened intently and jotted down on her clipboard a few notes on specific students.

In making their thoughts explicit, students examine their developing ideas.

TEACHER: Who has something they are wondering about?

STUDENT: I wonder how the Nanny met the dragon. I think that may be what this first picture is about.

TEACHER: Who has a theory about that?

Several theories were shared. Then the teacher directed the students to begin describing (in the whole group) and sketching (individually).

TEACHER: Now, sketchers, as you listen to the descriptions, remember that you can ask questions if you need more information, or tell us from time to time what you are thinking or drawing to guide us in our descriptions.

STUDENT: I see a creature — scaly, tall with long finger nails, and long toe nails too.

SKETCHER: Probably a dragon. Are there trees?

STUDENT: Yes, a pine and another.

SKETCHER: What is the dragon doing?

STUDENT: Might be roaring.

The students with the pictures worked to extract meaning from the pictures while the sketchers played with the ideas, raising their hands from time to time to ask for more information.

TEACHER: What shapes are your thoughts taking?

STUDENTS: I'm thinking of a huge creature, maybe with fire coming from its mouth.

I'm seeing the forest, hearing Dragonia and Nanny talking and I'm feeling worried for Nanny.

TEACHER: Would you like to see the picture? Notice when you compare your sketch with the original what other information would have been useful to you. What did you need to know?

STUDENT: I got the feeling of the dragon's size and some of the parts.

The students focus on 'what I need to know', not on 'what you did not tell me'.

The schemata for the story becomes more developed and allows new material an easy fit.

As the students compared their sketches both on paper and in their minds, she handed the text, opened to the second picture, to pairs in the opposite group, and blank paper to the original describers.

TEACHER: Let's start again in the same way. Sketchers, talk together and jot down any questions you have about the story. Describers, think of a good way to begin your descriptions. Focus on what you think the sketchers will need to know.

STUDENTS: We need to get a better idea of the forest.

I'd like to know more about the faces.

Students search for language which matches their visual thinking.

Again, for several minutes she jotted observational notes on the students at work then signalled for a halt in conversation.

TEACHER: What can you tell us about the second picture?

STUDENTS: They have diapers. They seem to be drinking from mega-bottles.

Scales and wings are on two baby dragons.

Teacher presses for the different possibilities, more than just one right answer.

SKETCHER: Baby dragons? Is the first dragon in the picture still?

TEACHER: If he says 'yes', what will that do to your thinking?

SKETCHER: Well, then I'll think that the baby dragons belong to it.

STUDENT: The first dragon isn't there.

TEACHER: So what are you thinking about now?

SKETCHER: Well, how do the little old lady, the baby dragons, and the big dragon all fit together?

I noticed a change in the language of the students in this second sharing. They asked more specific questions to gather details, and the words chosen in reply tended to be more specific. The drawings captured surprising details.

The class continued until each group had described twice and sketched twice. With each verbal-visual cycle, the students' language became more elaborate and more precise. This process seemed to require a great deal of energy and by the end of the fourth cycle, they were tiring.

TEACHER: I am impressed with your hard work today. Let me reflect for you on some of the things I noticed. Sometimes you seemed to be right inside the pictures finding words to make your thoughts clear. Other times you searched for words to help the sketchers see your thinking. Sketchers seemed to like hearing a jist statement first, and then asking very specific questions to get more information.

Turn to your partner and talk about what we did today and what you noticed about your thinking while we did it.

This personal reflection moves students towards more conscious control over their learning processes.

Please open your learning logs and show me what you noticed about your thinking today.

During the five minutes of writing, the teacher added more comments to her clipboard, describing specific students' participation in the strategy.

The teacher makes observations for the next learning sequence.

> Everything was easy, sort of in a way. I noticed that lots of people like this. I did. My thinking was busy.
>
> Josie (9 years)

> I noticed that my thinking was different from my partner's. At the beginning it was hard. I had too much to choose from what was in my head but near the end it got easier. I think I was thinking harder than usual.
>
> Tedmund (8 years)

I got more done today. My sketch was great! I asked a lot of questions. I could put my ideas into my picture. I really want to read the story. I had good ideas.

Susan (10 years)

TEACHER: I think we have just about worked ourselves out. Tomorrow we will read the author's version of *The Dragon Nanny* and see how our versions compare.

One Student's Sequence of Sketches

Extensions

1. Some teachers have the students write their own stories before hearing the author's version.

2. Bonnie Hartup, an early primary teacher, gathers her students around her in two groups and holds up the picture to just one group. She works with this group of students to give information to the other group which will help them 'paint the picture in their minds'. She models her own thinking out loud, then reverses roles in the groups. After hearing the story, the children move to centres to represent their understandings.

3. The use of the clipboard to record observational data on students' participation in a strategy during whole-group and small-group work is widely used by teachers. Many use a strategy-specific form which focuses on three or four students and three or four focus skills. Teachers are collecting data which indicates growth over time in a variety of contexts. These notes are then used as part of the portfolio of information from which the teacher clusters for her report card or for parent interviews.

Observation Form

Strategy: The Language of Pictures

Date: _____

Student	Clear description of main idea of picture	Focused questions	Use of story clip information in predictions
Josie			
Tedmund			
Susan			

LANGUAGE OF PICTURES: RECIPE

1. The teacher reads three to five story clips or excerpts from the text to the students.

2. Individually, students write their predictions after the teacher reads.

3. Students share predictions with one another.

4. Half of the class works with partners, views a picture from the story, and tells the other half of the class what they are viewing.

5. Teacher reviews with the students the components of a thought.

6. The second half of the class, in pairs, generates questions that they think will need to be answered, and prepares to sketch, individually, what they hear.

7. Sketchers are encouraged to ask questions to find out what they need to know.

8. Sketchers share their current thinking.

9. Students share the text's picture and change group roles.

10. The cycle is repeated until each student has described twice and sketched twice.

11. Students reflect in their learning logs.

12. The students read the author's version of the text to permit comparison.

10

Mapping the Big Ideas

The construction of concept maps causes students to personally reflect on the key concepts, or big ideas, of what they have been learning. *Mapping the Big Ideas* engages students in collaborative brainstorming of big ideas, small-group practice in linking and cross-linking big ideas, and individual reconstruction of the theme or topic based on 'what I know now'.

"... there should be frequent encouragement for students to develop their own organizing frameworks for the content of the program. Students should be taught how to create flowcharts, concept webs, relational diagrams, and to use other powerful tools for gaining an overview of the program's internal structure and a sense of sequence and progression."

— Milton McClaren, "A Curricular Perspective on the Principle of Understanding," in "Curriculum Towards Developing a Common Understanding."

"Cognitive maps . . . help students to represent abstract or implicit information in more concrete form, depict the relationships among facts and concepts, generate and elaborate ideas, relate new information to prior knowledge, and store and retrieve information."

— Jay McTighe and Frank T. Lyman, Jr., "Cueing Thinking in the Classroom: The Promise of Theory-Embedded Tools."

"A learner is only a partial biologist, for instance if he cannot read or write to discover information and meaning in biology. When a student takes the results of his or her observations about lobsters, reads, writes a draft, talks, reads, then writes again he or she learns what it is to think critically."

— J. Guthrie, *Excellence in Education.*

"In order to construct a hierarchical concept map, one must think through what one perceives to be the most inclusive, less inclusive, and least inclusive concepts in any body of subject matter. This requires active cognitive thinking . . . constructing a hierarchical concept map requires this kind of active integration of concepts . . . students report that this work 'really made them think', or helped them 'to see relationships they never saw before'."

— Joseph D. Novak and D. Bob Gowin, *Learning to Learn.*

TEACHER: What did you notice about your thinking as you clustered this morning?

STUDENTS: Very fast thinking and writing. Lots of images. I could feel the senses.

Lots of ideas. Each one kind of exploded into more ideas.

I focused on the topic we were talking about.

I got as many facts as I could. I could feel myself waiting for new information.

When I am clustering I notice that every thought leads to another thought. I think small, quick thoughts.

The students in this Grade 6/7 class had used **Clustering from Text** *to process a chapter in science. They sat in pods of four.*

TEACHER: Today we are going to be using our understandings in two ways. First, we'll write descriptive paragraphs and then we'll build concept maps. You will have new tools for shaping your thinking by the end of the morning. Look outside. Describe what you see.

STUDENTS: It's cold.

TEACHER: Think of a way to show me that it's cold. You told me it's cold. I need to be able to get a clear picture of coldness.

STUDENTS: Trees are bare.

Cheeks are rosy.

Noses are running as they brush the wind.

Murmurs of approval acknowledged a clear picture.

TEACHER: Tell us more.

STUDENTS: Car batteries wrestle to start.

Dust blows over ice-covered puddles.

TEACHER: What did you notice as the people reached for the words to show.

STUDENTS: I began to feel cold.

I heard the battery painfully turning.

My nose began to run.

The metacognitive chat helps students gain more conscious control of their thinking processes.

Strategies can be used for two purposes: to access and develop thinking and to shape thinking.

Teacher encourages students to build from first-hand experiences.

All responses are honored, but not ranked. This helps to create a risk-free climate for exploring ideas.

Everyone chuckled.

TEACHER: We really must have been giving your brain clear messages. I am now going to read a short image from your science text. Listen carefully and work with the thoughts.

> See the tarantula. . .
> Feel the fangs. . . exoskeleton. . .
> Notice the stinger. . . punctured abdomen. . .
> See the female. . . large. . .
> The male lighter. . .
> Notice the wasp and the sting. . .
> Feel the difficulties. . .
> Notice the venom. . . spider paralyzed. . .
> Feel the drag of the wasp. . . carrying. . .
> Hear the burrow. . . sealing. . .
> See eggs. . . hatching. . . spider alive. . .
> Notice mantis. . . feeding. . .
> See toads. . . tongue. . . feel the stickiness. . .
> Notice spiders eating. . .

Use of the image places students in the immediate content.

Play with your thoughts. When I count to three, turn to the people in your group and talk about what life is like for the spider.

The students' language animated the dangerous life. Laughter bubbled from their descriptions.

Articulating to a partner clarifies thinking and extends the connections.

TEACHER: Look at your cluster, play with the ideas, make connections, perhaps add a sketch. When you are ready, begin drafting to show the dangerous life of the tarantula.

The students concentrated, searching for words to match their thoughts. I noticed one boy quietly cheer from time to time when he thought of writing his account as a newscast. Students watched as the teacher modeled on the chalkboard. They wrote for about ten minutes, listened to a number of drafts, and reflected each time on what they noticed. The teacher asked them to listen for powerful expression. The teacher wrote the criteria on the board: action words, descriptive words, words that create emotions, tapping senses, sequence, humor. The students then wrote advice to themselves as 'Dear Me' notes, showing what they planned to do next time. They identified their most powerful parts.

The power of the process is reflected in the level of individual engagement.

Advice is personal editing for next time.

TEACHER: What did you notice about your own thinking?

STUDENTS: My thinking was almost non-stop ideas.

I learned more and I have a headache.

Very pressed, slow, focused thinking.

I felt like the throttle on my gas pedal was right on the floor.

When I am clustering I noticed that every thought leads to another thought.
I think small, quick thoughts.

The Hostile World
Of The Trancula

After the struggle the the ~~huge~~ female lies paralised, moving ever so slightly on the hard dirt floor. The female perces the trancula's abdomen with her sharp ~~fang~~ stinger. ~~of~~ The tranculas is not dead but paralised. After the long journey to the ~~spider~~ trancula den, the wasp dragging the huge trancula behind her, the female ~~deposeets~~ one, single, white egg on the trancula abdomen. ~~Later~~ she ~~buries~~ besries the trancula & the egg.
In a few ~~of~~ weeks, the egg ~~will~~ hatches & a tiny, white wormlike larva starts feeding on the trancula.

Very presed,
slow, focused thinking,

Dear me,
Next time put more action & senses into your story;
I think that the part ; "After the long journey...was the most ~~powerful~~ part.
Sincerly,
Me (Suzanne)

The recess bell ended the one-hour segment.

TEACHER: Think for a minute about the big ideas in that chapter, the important information about the spider's life. Talk to the people in your group and together brainstorm a list. What was that chapter about?

Teacher directs students to focus on content.

- the spider's hostile world
- enemies
- the hostile world of the tarantula
- paralyze
- cannabalistic
- larvae
- spiderlings
- hooks
- mating
- wasp
- build tunnel
- Black Widow can kill man
- lays eggs

- short life span
- nocturnal
- poison
- camouflage
- many enemies
- reproduction
- hair on legs
- prey
- hunt
- food chain
- suck juices
- tarantula hawk
- eats paralyzed spider

She wrote these big ideas on the board, then continued.

TEACHER: Look at the list we developed and with your group choose the most important idea, the biggest concept. What do you think is the biggest idea in this chapter?

STUDENTS: Enemies.

The teacher put 'enemies' to the right of the list at the top of the board. She crossed out 'many enemies' and asked them to identify another important idea.

STUDENTS: Camouflage.

She printed "camouflage" to the left and below "enemies," linking the two words with a line. Then she invited them to show how those two words might be related or connected.

Connections create a web of relationships in making meaning.

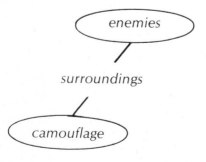

93

TEACHER: Think of a word that will show us how those two words connect. Connecting words helps us to make images, which are concepts.

STUDENT: Blend into surroundings.

TEACHER: If I put 'surroundings' on the line, would that create a picture?

The students nodded. The teacher crossed out "camouflage".

TEACHER: What is another important idea?

STUDENT: Nocturnal.

TEACHER: Does that relate to "camouflage" or would you like to start a new line of thinking?

STUDENT: Link it with "camouflage". I think the word might be "daytime" because they have to hide under rocks and leaves during the day. It could also link to "enemies" because they avoid enemies by moving around at night.

The teacher asked for a vote. The class decided to link it to 'enemies' with the word 'avoid'. The teacher crossed out 'nocturnal' and asked for another important idea.

To construct a class concept map, some majority rule decisions will be made.

TEACHER: There is no one right way to do a concept map. The map gives you a way to show where your understandings are unclear. You will find that after you play with the ideas two or three times your thinking will be very clear. The important thing is to work through the list until all of your ideas find a place. You will find that you may recall other information. That can be added anytime. The power of the map comes when you see ideas that you want to connect. We call that cross-linking. Can you see any places to cross-link on our beginning map.

The teacher emphasizes that a concept map is a personal representation of meaning.

Links and cross-links reveal sophisticated understanding.

STUDENTS: "Camouflage" and "nocturnal" with "hide in day."

Those two could be connected with "safe at night" too.

She added both cross-links.

TEACHER: Thank you. Your cross-links made me clearly see a picture. Usually we cross-link after we have fully developed the map.

I want you to work in pairs and build a map together. You will have an opportunity to make your own once we have practised the process. Reconstruct with your partner what you know about concept maps.

The process involves modeling and direct instruction, then collaborative group practice, then individual assignment.

94

She moved around the class giving out large sheets of paper (28 × 36 cm or 11 × 14''). The students clarified that there is no one right way, that linking words should create a picture, that the links should be as few words as possible, and that concept maps need to be constructed a few times to show detailed understandings.

Students recreate the task before beginning.

As the students worked, she spoke with individuals about how they were approaching the task. The externalizing of the thinking seemed to give new dimensions to the pairs. The students worked before deciding its placement. She encouraged them to experiment with their drafts and to notice their thinking as they worked. At the end of only half an hour they had a solid understanding of the structure.

Teacher scaffolds the learning by asking for clarification and elaboration. The interview is also a valuable evaluation tool.

TEACHER: You have worked for over two hours showing your thinking. We developed detailed criteria for description. Then you literally transformed your knowledge into another form by mapping your big ideas. I learned much about concept maps by watching your ideas develop. Thank you. Open your learning logs and jot down the important ideas about a concept map. We'll share our reflections after lunch. I want you to be able to try one at home tonight without the textbook. Tomorrow we'll discuss how many important skills are tucked into this process.

Logs written now are personal interpretations, a revisiting of the mapping process.

Feb 13   Russ

I focus on only the topic we're talking about.

bodies eats spider · cought before knowing · stung peri-lized · larva · wasp · spiders rest alot · Camoflosh · Enimies · do not live to old age · many enimies · fish · preying mantes · two front legs · toads · light body than girl · uses tough · have trouble finding spiders

95

This is Russ for channel ⑤ News and today we are doing Tarantula's. The tarantula is dangered by a wasp called A tarantula hawk witch charges it with it's stinger ready as the spider trys to fight back. feel the pain of the sting as the poison paralizes the tarantula, and working hard drags it to its home. See the larva eating the body of the tarantula.

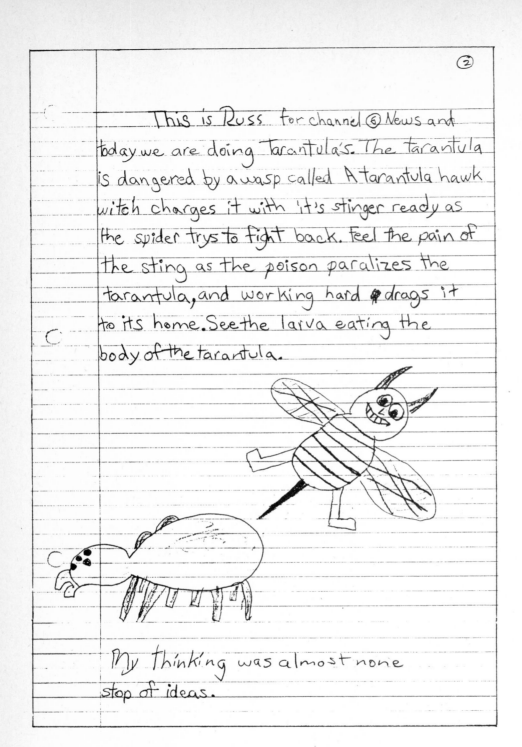

My thinking was almost none stop of ideas.

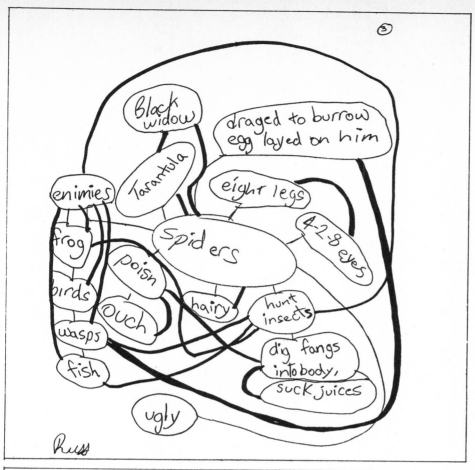

Russ

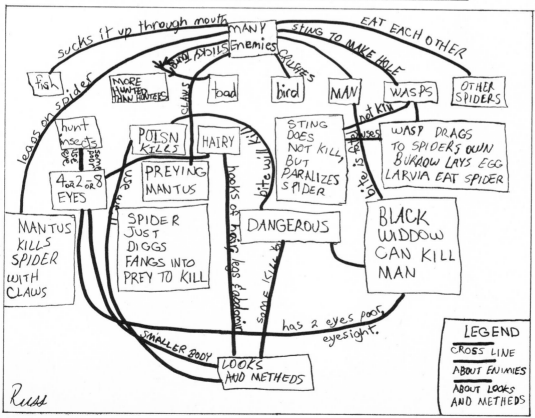

Russ

Extensions

1. In early primary the children work to paint the big ideas. Large circles are placed on the floor and connected with skipping ropes. The students are to show how the big ideas connect. Then they mount the circles on a wall and use wool to show connections. The students draw pictures or use word cards to show the many ways the big ideas connect.

2. Students are given a sheet of circles. They *draw* their big idea on one side of each circle and *write* the big idea on the other. They manipulate the circles studying the hierarchy in pictures, then turn them over to study the concepts in words. The students enjoy working with the two forms of expression. Moving the circles around enables them to construct the map many ways. They publish the circles, then invite their parents to come in and learn about their study. The parents watch the students construct a map as part of their portfolios of understandings.

3. Some teachers collect marks from concept maps. Each linking and cross-linking word gets one mark. The rationale is that these linking words show understandings. Maps can be judged as powerful, competent, and developing (Jeroski, et al, 1990). This criteria is developed with the student.

4. Maureen Dockendorf, a Burnaby consultant, uses the big curriculum content ideas to place in the circles. She links these ideas to build a theme.

MAPPING THE BIG IDEA: RECIPE

1. Read an image created from an experience, text, or topic sequence.

2. Talk to a partner about how it felt being 'in the topic'.

3. Exchange impressions with the entire class.

4. Write for five minutes to show, not tell, what has been learned.

5. Listen to drafts and build criteria for effective writing.

6. List the 'big ideas' of the text.

7. Choose two important ideas to begin the concept map.

8. Link these ideas with a word which shows the content of the text, the connection between the ideas, and/or an application of the information.

9. Map and link the 'big ideas', crossing out the ideas used as they are connected into the map.

10. Make cross-links between words.

11. Work with a partner or individually to list 'big ideas' and to create a concept map.

11

Editing Without Agony

In *Editing Without Agony*, students revisit a story or piece of text to deepen the understanding necessary for powerful writing. After drafting a written response, students listen in role to develop criteria for effective communication, considering form, purpose, and audience. The second draft is written collaboratively, the third, individually. Over time, students internalize criteria for powerful writing.

"... they have been active participants in the creation of meaning. This process allows them to play, gives them permission to improvise, to produce idiosyncratic responses, to become emotionally involved, in short, to interact with content in highly creative ways. Every new idea to be learned requires rediscovery by the learner, or as Piaget observed, 'For anyone truly to learn something for himself, he must recreate it for himself.' "

— Gabriele Lusser Rico, "Daedalus and Icarus Within: The Literature/ Art/Writing Connection."

"A democratic society needs people who have the linguistic abilities which will enable them to discuss, evaluate, and make sense of what they are told, as well as to take effective action on the basis of their understanding."

— J. Kingman, "Report of the Committee of Inquiry into the Teaching of English Language."

"Inquiry focuses students' attention on strategies for transforming raw data . . . students might express personal experience vividly, examine sets of data to develop and support explanatory generalizations or analyze situations that present problems and develop arguments about those situations. On the average, these treatments are three-and-a-half times more effective than a traditional study of model pieces of writing."

— George Hillocks, Jr., *Synthesis of Research on Teaching Writing.*

"Response rests on time and choice. We respond to topics students choose and by responding, we teach. Thus, we teach writing from students' drafts."

— Jane Hansen, *When Writers Read.*

TEACHER: Can you think of a time when you tried to persuade someone to do something? Perhaps you wanted to go somewhere special or maybe you wanted a special treat. Turn to your partner and talk about what you did to persuade someone to do something for you.

Provincial assessment results indicate that students need more practice in persuasive writing. (British Columbia, 1988)

The six- and seven-year-olds' eyes flashed with recognition. The partners huddled together sharing their experiences. The teacher had grouped active students with active students and quiet students with quiet students. I had not seen this approach to grouping before and I was fascinated by their quick engagement.

TEACHER: Let's talk about what works when you are trying to persuade someone to do something. Who has an idea?

STUDENTS: When I want something from my brother I try to give him something first.

The students are drawing on real-life experience.

I say, ''Please, please, please.''

I keep asking my Mom until she gives it to me.

Well now, [pause] I start saying nice things about my Daddy and he says yes.

The students delighted in hearing each others' approaches. The teacher extended each idea by inviting the students to name the approach that worked. She developed a list on the board:

- *making a deal*
- *begging*
- *pestering*
- *flattering*
- *whining*
- *threatening*
- *offering to help*

TEACHER: Yesterday I told you a story that I had heard called ''Why the Woodpecker Has a Long Beak.'' This morning we will use our thinking from that story to help us learn more about persuading.''

The teacher moves from strategies which develop thinking to those which shape thinking to form.

*The students had processed the story using the **Reading Like an Expert** strategy. With each of the four sections of the text they had orally questioned, summarized, and clarified. They wrote their predictions on **Thinking Papers.***

TEACHER: I will read some thoughts from the story to help you remember. Put yourself in a comfortable thinking position.

The teacher began to slowly read a series of images and I began tracking two students. The teacher had given me a form on which to focus my observations.

TEACHER:

Image helps memory
retrieval.

> See yourself in the forest. . .
> Notice the old woman. . .curious,
>   poking around. . .eavesdropping. . .making mischief. . .
> See the mayor. . .
> Feel the ants in the sack. . .
> Hear the mayor talking to the woman. . .
> Notice his warning. . .
> Hear the woman's promise. . .
> See the old woman trotting home. . .
>   fingers twitching. . . in the field. . .
>
> Notice the ants escaping, running, hiding, burrowing. . .
>
> See the woman gathering. . . packing. . . scrambling after. . .

When I count to three, talk to your partner about what it was like to be an ant escaping from the bag. One. . . two. . . three.

Students speak of the
experience as insiders.

Everyone slipped into the role of ants easily. The students I was observing described their hiding places in vivid detail. The teacher waited for a lull in the conversations before signaling an end to the dialogue. She moved into the groups of students in role as an interviewer.

TEACHER: Excuse me, can you tell us what happened to you when the bag opened?

STUDENTS: I ran and I climbed under some moss to hide.

   I'm up a tree. No way she's going to get me.

   I hid right in a hole.

The teacher walked up to individual students, engaging them in conversations about their places of refuge. The responses brought the scene to life.

Teacher adopts a role to
maintain the seriouness.

TEACHER: I wonder how the old woman is feeling right now. What might she be thinking about?

STUDENTS: She's [pause] in trouble.

   Yes, she's scared. The mayor is going to find out.

   She'll be a woodpecker forever now.

TEACHER: So you think she's pretty worried.

The heads nodded seriously.

TEACHER: What do we know about the old woman?

The teacher is establishing
audience,

103

STUDENTS: She doesn't have many friends.

She breaks promises.

And she's upset now.

The teacher paused, showing deep concern about this situation.

TEACHER: Ants, I know the old woman will be here any minute. She'll be wanting to gather you up. Think of some way to persuade her to let you go free. Share your ideas with your partner.

— establishing purpose,

After the students had had a few minutes of animated discussion, the teacher invited them to cluster and draft a letter to the old woman. They wrote for seven minutes before they began listening to the pleas.

— establishing form.

TEACHER: As you listen to the ants' ideas, I want you to think like the old woman. See if the ideas work on you. Put your thumb up if you are convinced.

STUDENT: Dear woman, I don't want to get caught because I can't breathe in the sack. That's why. I want to be with my friends. I can't move around in there.

Three thumbs went up. The teacher invited the students to tell why they were convinced. She wrote the ideas in point form on the board.

Students substantiate their thinking.

- *It's mean to squish them.*
- *They should be allowed to be free.*
- *Ants have friends.*

STUDENT: Dear old woman, don't get me because I bite hard.

Everyone giggled, but no thumbs went up. The students explained that a little ant bite wouldn't worry this old lady. One student reflected that biting is mean.

STUDENT: Dear old woman, I want to be free and all our friends including the insects that eat us and the ones we eat. I am helpful and eat the insects that eat your plants and if I am put in the bag, I will not be able to help you.

The student spoke emphatically. Heads nodded and many thumbs went up this time. The teacher invited students to elaborate on why they were convinced. You could feel the momentum of the criteria for arguments building. Two more drafts were read and discussed.

Criteria for arguments develop through the experience in role as the old woman.

TEACHER: Do you think any of the ways we first listed on the board would work on the old woman?

The teacher pointed to each approach. Heads nodded in agreement or shook in disagreement. She invited them to explain why the possibility

The teacher is matching approach to audience.

would or would not work. Their reasons reflected a solid under-standing of persuasion. The teacher crossed out the ones they rejected.

TEACHER: Are there any other ways to persuade that we should add to our list?

The teacher added their suggestions to the list.

- *Speaking nicely*   - *Giving reasons*

TEACHER: You listened so thoughtfully this morning. You were able to tell why the arguments might work. Now I would like you to work with your partner to draft a new letter to the old woman. You may use any ideas that come to you. Talk first, cluster your ideas, then write a new letter together.

Collaboration after a group sharing is a form of editing.

The two students I was observing huddled together almost whispering. One began writing while the other advised. They read over their first drafts only once. The talk seemed to bring their ideas together.

The talk is negotiating the content.

After ten minutes, the students assumed the role of the old lady again to listen to the new drafts. They worked to articulate what was convincing in each piece.

Listening in role sharpens audience sensitivity.

TEACHER: You have worked hard on your persuading this morning. Let's look back at what we did and why we did it. What did we do first?

The teacher recorded the critical elements in a class learning log. I collected the drafts, eager to see the expression in the two pieces of writing. At the end of the sequence after they had actually written three times, I planned to document the growth.

Authentic assessment reflects growth over time.

Extensions

1. The next day the teacher imaged the story again and the students each wrote a third draft. Notice Chris's development as he progressed from his initial thinking paper through to the third draft. (Chris is six years old.)

From Thinking Paper (Predictions) to Third Draft

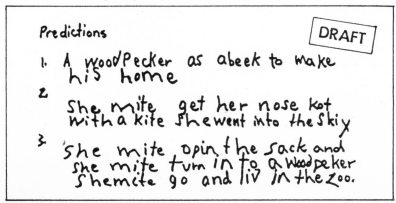

Deer woomin I dunt wont to get
cot becus I cat brees in the sack.
Thans wiy I to be with my frens
I cant moov around in ther

DRAFT

Dear old woman you shund let us free becus
we a the insekes that et your
flowers. So we would let us
liv whith are family. If you don't
let us go we will bete up your
hus and your cow and your
dog and your shark and
your snake and then
we will askap and liv in peas

DRAFT

DRAFT

Dear old woman.
I need to go be in nature.
I rely need to to go home
Please Let me go. I
command you to let
me go now   so now I will
be going now.
I will do anything for you
if you let me go. I can go.
I thank you very much. No
my family will say "Hurray." I
will say good bye. You can
come visit us any time
when you need frinds.
yrous truly, chris

106

2. Observations on two students, Chris and Ryan, appear on the observation form for the strategy **Editing Persuasion**. A blank copy of this form is provided for your use.

Teachers who prefer to record observations on two or more students on the same form would follow the format illustrated on page 67.

Observation Form

Strategy: Editing Persuasion

Student's Name: _____ Chris _____ Date/s: _____

Interaction	Draft 1	Draft 2	Draft 3
• giggled as he talked in role • elaborated details of his hiding place • listened to his partner and compared his ideas to his partner's ideas • reflected to whole class how the old woman was feeling • read draft to class • collaborated with assistance • stayed in at recess to write • persuaded partner to stay in	• showed consequences • related ideas to audience • stated main idea • word choice clear • voice apparent	• uses 'we' • expanded reasons • sense of writer's voice is apparent • used threat to argue • clear statement of position • conclusion	• clear sense of audience • clear statement of position • clear, fluent • main ideas treated with emphasis • supporting details carefully chosen • varied his approach • varied sentence length • quantity reflects content

Comments: _____
_____
_____
_____
_____

Observation Form

Strategy: Editing Persuasion

Student's Name: _____ Ryan _____ Date/s: _____

Interaction	Draft 1	Draft 2	Draft 3
• seemed to mirror partner's actions • talked about hiding place • drew it on his desk • never stopped moving • looked at each person speaking; built on two people's ideas • coached partner to work with him • pointed to his first draft reflecting an idea he thought worked • wrote draft pouring over each word	• ideas expressed as narrative • writing is clear, fluent sequence of statements • original ideas • sense of voice	• uses 'we' • moved into persuasive form • main ideas stated • awareness of implications • sense of audience • original ''we are two vishis praying mantis''	• clear statement of position and line of thought is sustained and convincing • word choice is appropriate, lively, specific • ideas relate to audience • sense of voice clear

Comments: _____
_____
_____
_____
_____
_____

3. Eight months later Chris's teacher, Nance Charron, sent us his journal entry. He was responding to, ''You are a mouse caught by a lion. Persuade him to let you go,'' before reading *The Lion and the Mouse*. She reflected, ''I believe the woodpecker lesson is still with them, even after all this time!''

> Journal
> "why, why Mr. lion? why do you want me?" I'm only skin and bonse. Please let me go. I'm only fifteen. I'm a teenajer. I need to go home at 7:00 and my bed time is 8:00 and I'll give you a bak of twix and a life supplie of corn chips and root bear and coke. My mother will be mad if I'm home after 8:00 and mom will take her woodn' spoon and smak me and I'll never be abl to ride my bike and I really like to ride ride it again all rite?
> Chris
> DRAFT

4. Each time we use this process we feel the agony of editing disappear. By developing criteria through the students' own expression, we notice tremendous development in short periods of time. Notice Todd, a Grade 7 student, as he writes:

- in response to, ''Why do you think the woodpecker has a long beak?''

> **Todd**
>
> I believe the woodpecker has a long beak because he uses it to make holes to sleep in—to dig for—for old defense

- to ask questions before reading:

> Where did they come from?
> Are they brought here—or do they fly here?
>
> ? Why does he have it?
> How long have they ixsisted for?

- a first draft to persuade:

> Dear (Old) Woman
>
> Please don't put me in the bag because I have a highly contagious disease and I don't want you to catch it. but I don't mind if you put my friends in. they're mean anyway. If your nice you wont put me in the sack. the disease is one you don't want to get I can't quite remember what it is called but it is very harmfull.

- advice to himself after listening in role and developing criteria:

> don't be sarcastic
> ~~but~~ use flattery
> in a way it would
> not seem sarcastic
> discover her likes and
> dislikes - to flatter
> her with

- a letter to the mayor, in the role of the old woman, explaining why he let the ants go:

> Mr. Man
>   You got your job for many reasons. One was because you were understanding and kind. I've hurt so many people in my life. I could not hurt anymore. Please don't do anything drastic that you might regret. I don't know why I am so nosy I guess its because I have no friends. But I had to let these ants go because they said they would be my friends. I realize I failed you but for once in my life I haven't failed myself.
>   Yours Truly
>   The Old Lady

- a reflection on how his thinking had changed:

> My thinking has changed because I have taken what other people think into consideration.

Developing criteria with the students enables them to under-stand their own growth. When they learn to identify criteria for a specific form of writing, they are able to reflect on their own text and give themselves advice. Each cycle through this process offers new possibilities for expression.

5. To assess:

   - Have the students develop an argument in a ten-minute writing period.
   - Ask them how many pieces of evidence a powerful argument might have.
   - Ask them what strong evidence sounds like. List the begin-ning set of criteria on the board.
   - Listen to a number of drafts, reflecting each time. Focus on what developed evidence sounds like.
   - Have the students mark the places where they have shown evidence.

   This is one process that enables students to know criteria for successful expression. The process is exactly the same for description and narration.

   - Students might write, listen to identify attributes of powerful expression, reflect personally, share with a group, and draft again.

6. Another approach begins with students studying a model. The students might read a newspaper editorial and develop criteria together. They might then gather facts and turn the facts into an article using a collaborative process.

EDITING WITHOUT AGONY: RECIPE

1. Teacher begins by processing a story, or piece of text, that contains an issue.

2. The next day, students discuss how they persuade at home.

3. Teacher lists different persuasive approaches on the chalkboard.

4. Teacher reads an "image" from the story.

5. Teacher, in role, interviews the students.

6. Teacher and students decide on the audience for the persuading.

7. Students draft a letter individually.

8. Students listen in opposite role to test arguments and signal if they are convinced.

9. Criteria are developed through the student drafts.

10. Students elaborate on why they are or are not convinced.

11. Students draft collaboratively, listen for convincing arguments, elaborate again, and refine criteria.

12. Students reflect on their own arguments, possibly offering advice.

13. Students listen to the "image" again.

14. Students write a third draft.

15. Students reflect on what they noticed about their own learning.

12

Becoming Researchers

Becoming Researchers makes explicit a process to lead students into forming their own inquiry questions, investigating data on these questions, and presenting their findings in a concise format. Several other strategies weave into this extended sequence. Students work with the whole class in modeling and direct instruction, in collaborative groups, and individually for their final report.

"The classroom where students are using their language to come to terms with new information, to make sense of it so that it can become their own, is the context in which the most effective learning will take place. . . ."

— Jo-Anne Reid, Peter Forrestal and Jonathan Cook, *Small Group Learning in the Classroom.*

"Process, on the other hand, is not just method; it is learning how to manipulate content in order to extend its relationships. It is an exploration of the ways we learn and internalize content and how we might apply these to produce meaningful understandings of ourselves and our world."

— Sam Crowell, *A New Way of Thinking: The Challenge of the Future.*

"Instructional improvement is a constant cycle of decisions, discoveries, and further decisions, as we explore the unknown."

— Carl Glickman, "Unlocking school reform: Uncertainty as a condition of professionalism," *Kappan.*

"The children's own purposes, meanings and intentions were the starting point. Those often were embedded in their active and social involvement in projects that the teacher had planned and the children had made their own."

— Nancy G. Platt, "What Teachers and Children Do in a Language Rich Classroom."

TEACHER: Boys and girls, Mrs. Wiebe, our teacher-librarian and I will be working together with you today. We'll be starting to work on a report, to gather information and to organize it. Any guesses what the topic might be?

The room has been decorated in space images for over a week. Every library book we could find on the subject lined shelves or stood on small tables. Students had browsed through the many appealing volumes. Needless to say, they chorused, "Space!"

Two days earlier the class had brainstormed questions they had relating to the subject. A chart recorded their questions.

> Is it true space keeps going on and on?
> What are stars really like?
> Are there aliens?
> Could aliens come from other planets near ours?
> How did it all begin, in the first place?

These were very general questions, hardly specific enough to begin a report.

Just the day before, the class had done a huge cluster — "What we know about space." Some students knew a surprising amount, much more than the teacher. Still, the group's pooled knowledge pointed to the need to immerse them in facts about space before they could isolate a question for study.

The cluster had been tacked up at the back of the classroom.

Both teachers felt dissatisfied with the way in which they'd taught research skills formerly. This working together was to be an attempt to combine aspects of each other's methodology. From planning together they'd already decided to be experimental — to drop an idea that wasn't working and plan further. The first joint decision was to lead students to develop a question that they really wanted an answer to. We didn't want the inquiry to be a summary put into their own words but devoid of a personal need to know.

*The 'what do you wonder about' and 'what do you know' exercises suggested a teacher intervention to bring about more specific questions. Because the reading levels spanned ten grades in the one Grade 5/6 room, a decision to do a **Jigsaw Strategy** at this point required the teachers to track down material suitable for all students. Four articles were selected, one from a primary level about the solar system to the final complex one from World Book Encyclopedia. Students were divided by ability to read the text, forming four expert groups. They were directed to highlight five or six pieces of information they considered interesting in the articles they read. This they would attempt to agree on in their groups.*

By working collaboratively with classroom teachers, the librarian reinforces the idea that he or she is a teacher, too.

Students are invited in before the actual lessons begin.

Space had been one of the topics students requested when on the first day of school the class generated a list of what they really hoped to learn about this year.

Visible records of the thinking expressed are prominently displayed.

The collaborative planning engaged the teachers in an excitement of their own. Both acknowledged changes to their thinking as a result of talking together.

As learners, teachers also read and attend workshops. **Jigsaw Strategy** *we learned from Cooperative Learning.*

Eagerly students anticipated using the brightly colored highlighters and headed to designated areas with their articles. Groups performed the tasks in various ways. Two had an obvious good reader read orally, while the rest followed and interjected when someone thought a fact interesting. Other groups took turns reading paragraphs to proceed through the information. Interestingly the very able readers read through their articles alone, silently before discussing points to note. The class had done cooperative activities before so they understood individual accountability. After twenty minutes or so the groups were directed to compose sharing arrangements with four students, one from each expert group.

In these groups the students "taught" their article, discussing the points the expert group had highlighted. We noted no hesitancy or sense of difference among group members, regardless of the degree of difficulty of their information. On the contrary, animated discussions arose in each group with most students contributing orally. Less verbal students appeared just as interested and involved. In the group interesting facts were recorded on cards to be brought to the whole session.

Returning to the front board where masking tape was on hand, we categorized the cards that represented student interests. Four categories emerged as areas for possible investigation.

Space Shuttles	Planets Jupiter Saturn	Life on Other Planets	Black Holes

We then turned the category names into questions.

- *What are the special features of space shuttles?*
- *Is there life on other planets?*
- *What is the planet Jupiter like? (Saturn)*
- *What is a black hole?*

We concluded the lesson by asking students to think which question they would most like to work on and to be prepared with their decision for the next day.

During a planning session we decided at this point to have the students search for their own information relating to their chosen question. We referred them to table of contents and indexes as aids to locate the required facts. Some worked with partners; others read alone for the whole period, jotting bits of information as they read. We recognized a need for students to be more familiar with their own questions before they could narrow the field to just a few areas for their report.

To model a way to do this narrowing, we again did a group **Brainstorm-Categorize** *of questions that could be answered within one*

Limiting the individual topic choices until the students are familiar with the process is essential.

topic, "What are space shuttles?" Since half the class had selected this as their interest, the questions were many.

Is the shuttle capable of orbiting the moon?
What is the weight of the external tank?
How can it land again?
How does it take off from the moon?
How many controls are there on it?
How fast is it going when it lands?
How does a shuttle do a 180° pivot?
How long can it stay in space?
How fast does it move compared to a jet?
Does the amount of fuel depend on how far it is going?
How does gravity let it get into space?
How does the tank break away?
Why did the Challenger disaster happen?
How does it withstand heat coming back to Earth?
How long does it take to build?

As the questions were categorized, significant features emerged as important to include in a report. For space shuttles the categorizing resulted in the following questions.

Shuttles

1. What are the special features of a space shuttle?
2. What ground work is needed?
3. What are the expeditions the space shuttle has made?
4. How does the space shuttle lift off and land from space and from Earth?

Samples of Student Fact Sheets

How does the shuttle lift off and land?
- rocket boosters send off thrust
- lands at speed of 200 mph on runway
- SRB's dislodge after 2 min of flight
- ET falls after 4 min of flight
- wheel gear doors open
- positioned upright for flight
- launch pad falls back
- retro roks rocket fire
- take off thrust is 6.125000 lbs
- 3 stages
- 180° pivot
- challenger blew up
- glides

B. Question: What ground work is needed
- maintenence
- re-tiling
- cleaning
- re-fueling
- welding
- painting
- attachin SRB's, ET to shuttle
- loading onto crawler
- loading supplies
- make nose cone + fuel tank
- tracking shuttle in missioncontrol
- unloading leftover suplies
- safty checks made
- flight prep.

Question- What are the explorations the shuttle has made
- orbits earth
- sends out satellites
- takes photos
- Canada arm prepairs satellites
- carry payload-65,000lbs
- space lab
- work on space shuttles stations
- mission to space stations
- dislodging satellites
- blowing up satellites
- bring satellites back to earth

The students researching shuttles proceeded with four different colored fact sheets to gather information. Facts relating to one question were recorded on sheets of one color. The teachers then circulated to help students interested in other topics categorize questions and arrive at what they considered key points to be discussed to answer each question. Once the questions had been decided and listed, these students recorded them on fact sheets in the same way that the space shuttle investigators had done. They then set forth to find information to record under each question. This activity required two forty-minute blocks before students had gathered sufficient information.

We decided in our planning that while some students had the idea of facts that would support a good exploration, others didn't. At this point we thought that working together in groups to choose among all the facts recorded and come up with one large planning chart from which to generate a report might just work.

Students worked in groups, discussing facts and arriving at what seemed most important to them. Each group developed their collective sheet, selecting only six facts from all those gathered on the fact sheets.

We learned this from workshops when we first started to learn new ways to do research from Richmond teachers Borman, Hunter, and Mikituk.

Real inquiry takes time.

Staying open to alternative routes allows teachers their own ongoing research into effective practice.

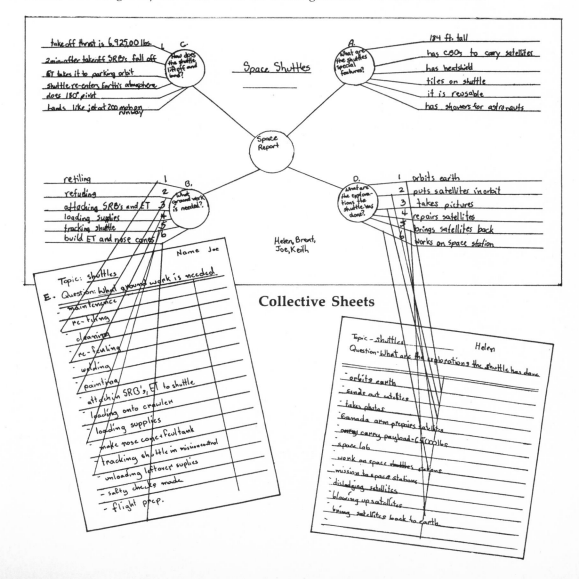

Collective Sheets

The teacher-librarian and I were pleased with the results: the filled-in sheets, the high interest, and the largely cooperative response of the groups.

Still, we realized this wasn't all there was to report writing, making up outlines and stringing the facts together. Could we allow the time to model for and with the whole group how to write an interesting report? Where to from here?

TEACHER: Class, your teachers have been talking about how to help you from here. Since many of you are doing space shuttles, we thought we'd develop a report together, noticing how ideas are introduced and tied together and how to keep the reader interested.

Begin to think like a reader. Which question would you want answered first? Which question on your planning sheet would best introduce your topic? In your groups, put a letter from A to D in front of each question you'll be answering. When you finish that, begin reading the facts under each question and decide which of the facts would come first, second, etc. up to six.

The groups did this activity faster than we had anticipated and returned to the desk area.

TEACHER: Would one of the space shuttle groups let us use their planning sheet?

One is offered and quickly run off as an overhead. Two overhead projectors were used with students sitting in a semicircle.

TEACHER: Under special features of the space shuttle, this group has six points listed. What are we going to have to do with these facts in order to make them interesting to other people, our readers?

STUDENT: Make an interesting paragraph.

TEACHER: What is it Asimov does? Listen to this line and tell me if it's a good way to start: ''There's no doubt about it . . . the moon is. . . .'' Do you like it? What do you like about it?

Modeling from good sources is second nature.

STUDENTS: It's got zing.

It draws you into the paragraph.

TEACHER: Remember, right now we're leaving the opening paragraph until later. We're just working on one of the paragraphs that develops the facts you selected as important. That's the paragraph on special features. The first point is: It is reusable. How could that be said?

STUDENT: After a shuttle comes down from its orbit you may think it is scrapped, but you will find out differently.

TEACHER: What do you think of that as a beginning?

STUDENT: [Nods.] That's good.

TEACHER: What might the next line be?

STUDENTS: Well, when the shuttle lands you. . . I can't think of anymore.

When the shuttle lifts off, the rocket boosters fall off two minutes later. After six minutes, the external tanks fall off and explode.

TEACHER: How many of you think these details are wanted?

STUDENT: I don't think so. We could use them in ''lift off and land.''

TEACHER: Then what could come next?

STUDENT: The shuttle is a reusable aircraft that takes off like a rocket and lands like an airplane.

TEACHER: Let's read the two sentences out loud, together. That sounds great. [Nods.] Could you read the next point, Julien?

STUDENT: Has special heat rejection panels.

TEACHER: Thank you, Julien. How can we build a ladder to the other sentences?

STUDENTS: One special feature.

I think another special feature ties it together better.

How about ''Another special feature is the heat shield.''

Yes, that's short and sweet. [Laughter]

TEACHER: All right, what's next?

STUDENT: This unique shield has thousands of tiny tiles that are made from 99% silica fibres.

TEACHER: Good. This is really coming. I see you are adding from what you know to each point, which is really just a skeleton outline, isn't it? Now turn to the person beside you and come up with the sentence that you would use next.

STUDENTS: The heat shield is the shuttle's protector so it won't burn up during re-entry.

The tiles are made so the shuttle won't burn up as it re-enters Earth's atmosphere.

How about change the first suggestion to ''won't burn up in Earth's atmosphere''?

Or ''won't burn up on re-entry into Earth's atmosphere.''

Class settles on this composite.

TEACHER: Let's all read together what we've written so far. Good, and the next point.

STUDENT: Most powerful engine built.

By suggestions, challenges, and votes we arrive at ''Another feature of this sophisticated craft is that it has the most powerful engine ever built. The large group writing together is exacting. There are so many possibilities offered. We were excited by the concentration required and given by these ten- and eleven-year-olds. We proceeded through six lessons of writing a shuttle report. By this point the groups wanted to be turned loose, to see what they could come up with. A few preferred to work alone, but most headed for the spaces we found for them in the library, the hall, the book room, and in the classroom. Sentence by sentence they carved out their reports. The process allowed the able students to help the developing ones. The report belonged to them all. The time had been worth it.

Allowing students this choice is comfortable for everyone.

I thought back to a statement by Schulman that we should slow down in schools so that learning could become deeper and more collaborative, that we should study fewer topics with greater care and collaborative deliberation, to recapture both pace and time.

The students proved themselves more capable than we'd ever have guessed. The teachers, through trusting what was needed next, even though the modeling, for instance, took a lot of time, created a process that worked for these particular students.

Modeling the writing with the class acknowledges that writing is indeed messy.

The reports in draft form were transferred to computer disks where students worked to come up with their own introduction and conclusion for the report they'd done together, as well as to revise points they wanted to convey differently from how the group had expressed them.

The finished reports were made into books, complete with illustrations, dedication, table of contents, bibliography, and a final page with a photograph and write-up about the author. The books were carded and shelved in the library for other classes to sign out. A reverence took hold of the class as the finished reports looked so professional and bore the name of each of them as the author.

SAMPLE REPORT

I dedicate this report to Devin, Cory, and Jason for all their help in helping me find facts and helping me to draw the Canada Arm. I also dedicate this book to Harrison Ford for inspiring me and getting me to write the best I could.

Space Shuttles

The space shuttle is a reusable space craft which stands at a height of approximately one hundred and eighty-four feet tall. The two things that are reusable are the space shuttle itself and the solid rocket boosters that are attached to the external tank (ET), which is not reusable.

Some of the tiles on the shuttle's body are used as a heat shield so the shuttle can enter Earth's atmosphere safely. The tiles are made from 99% silica fibers and cover most of the shuttle's body.

The shuttle has the most powerful engines ever built for a spacecraft. It has three F-5 engines and two small oms engines. These unique F-5 engines are used to take the shuttle into a higher orbit. The oms engines are used to keep the shuttle circling Earth. The heat shield is the shuttle's protector so that it won't blow up on re-entry into Earth's atmosphere. Over one thousand tiles make up the shuttle's heat shield. If some of the tiles fall off the shield turns blue-white instead of red-orange. The flaps on the wings and tail are used for steering the shuttle towards the runway. The wing flaps are moved up and down while the tail flaps are moved left to right.

A few days before lift-off, the shuttle is loaded with supplies such as: food, water, towels, oxygen, soap, reading materials, scientific recording materials, etc. Before the shuttle is loaded onto the crawler it is refueled with rocket fuel. Then it is taken to the launch pad. Before the shuttle takes off it is positioned upright on its S.R.B.'s (solid rocket boosters) for flight. The thrust given by the solid rocket boosters is two million pounds. After two minutes of flight the S.R.B.'s fall off. After six minutes the ET falls and disintegrates. A shuttle enters Earth's atmosphere backwards and does a 180° pivot to direct it towards the runway. When a shuttle lifts off it is tracked and monitored in mission control until it lands. After the shuttle comes down from space, it gets towed to the vehicle bay for repair. One of the main repairs needed is retiling. On re-entry some of the tiles may fall off and need replacing.

One of the explorations the space shuttle has done is orbit Earth. It can stay in orbit for about one month. While in space the shuttle can take photos two different ways. One is by the portable camera on the M.M.U. (manned manoeuvring unit). The other is by satellite. These photos are used for scientific purposes, postcards and posters.

Helen C. (11 years)

THE
SPACE
SHUTTLE

BY: HELEN
COATES

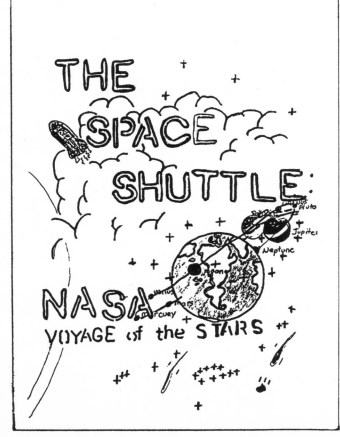

BECOMING RESEARCHERS: RECIPE

1. Surround students with resources.

2. Brainstorm "What do you wonder about?" on topic.

3. Brainstorm "What do you know?" on topic.

4. "Jigsaw" with information at suitable reading levels.

5. Highlight five or six interesting facts in Jigsaw groups. Record these facts on to cards.

6. Categorize facts on cards together as whole class.

7. Turn resulting category names into questions. Decide for next day what question to work on.

8. To narrow topic, brainstorm-categorize the chosen question within each group. Turn resulting category names into questions.

9. Copy questions on to fact sheets — one question on each colored fact sheet.

10. Research questions individually, recording on to sheets.

11. Ask groups to select together the six most important facts for each question. Have students fill in planning sheet as a group.

12. Number the order of paragraphs.
    Number the order of sentences.
    To begin modeling, read from good example of expository writing.

13. Model writing a paragraph — how to tie sentences together
    — how to get and keep audience interest.

14. Work together in same groups around a blackboard space, using planning sheet from which to generate sentences and paragraphs. Copy resulting writing by the group on to paper.

15. Model writing introductions.

16. Students each write their own introduction to group report.

17. Model writing conclusion.

18. Have students write their own conclusions to the group report.

19. Publish reports — revise, edit, proofread, illustrate.

20. Present to librarian.

13

Think of a Time 1-2-3

The *Think of a Time 1, 2, 3* strategy is modeled with a parent meeting. Using a focus question, parents (or students) in triads examine a concept from three different points of view: as participant, as witness, as causal agent. After each point of view, shared understandings are constructed using the knowledge of the whole group. Finally, critical attributes of the concept are identified.

". . . for students to attain personal mastery of key concepts and vital skills requires practice, reflection, discussion, applications to a wide range of different contexts and settings, and conversion to the students' own language and systems of representation. . . ."

— Milton McClaren, "A Curricular Perspective on the Principle of Understanding in Curriculum."

"The child's self-concept is the most important single factor affecting all behavior and, perhaps more than anything else, determines how successful the experience of school will be. . . ."

— Barry Dwyer, *Parents, Teachers, Partners.*

"Parents whose children have worked with teachers who incorporate co-operative small groups into their classroom programs are very supportive. . . parents feel very strongly that their children should learn skills which will be required in their future occupations."

— Judy Clarke, Ron Wideman, and Susan Eadie, *Together We Learn.*

"Teachers need to set up an environment and a range of experiences that ensures that talking, reading and writing (and other forms of representation) play a vital part in all learning. They need to talk with children while they are engaged with learning. . . ."

— Moira McKenzie, "Classroom Contexts for Language and Literacy."

TEACHER: Thank you for coming out to this parent workshop on student self-concept. In the needs assessment you filled out, this topic was given the top priority. What worries you most about self-esteem? Turn to the person beside you and talk about your concerns.

The room grew lively with talk. Voices and gestures amplified their concerns.

TEACHER: Thank you for such energetic responses. What were some of your concerns?

PARENTS: I want my children to feel confident enough to make their own decisions. I don't want them to be swayed by peer pressure.

I look at my son and I want him to feel good about himself. I work in an employment office and the biggest problem we see is people who seem to lack self-confidence.

People who feel good about themselves seem to think in any situation. They seem to be more flexible and easier to be with. I want my child to be able to get along with others, listen to others' ideas, and feel confident enough to offer his own point of view.

TEACHER: Thank you. Those concerns are important. Our society reflects many problems that can be traced back to low self-esteem. As parents and teachers we have many opportunities to help children build their confidence. Let's get inside the idea of self-concept through our own experiences. To do this we will use a process we call **Think of a Time 1-2-3.** This is a strategy that we also use in teaching children.

I have arranged your seats in groups of three. First, please number yourselves 1, 2, or 3. I want you all to think of a time when someone boosted your self-esteem and I would like you to share this in your triad. Next we will share some of the ideas with the whole group. Then the number 1 person will stand and move to a new group. We will do this three times. Then everyone will return to the original seats. Let me model it for you.

She walked over to a threesome and talked to them.

TEACHER: Decide on which number you are.

Giggles erupted as they pointed at each other.

TEACHER: Think of a time when someone boosted your self-esteem. Each of you share an experience.

The teacher identifies the reason for the topic chosen.

Involvement honors the fact that all parents are there because they have a question or a concern.

Seating is arranged to be inclusive and non-threatening.

Modeling with a group encourages all the parent groups to start.

She turned to the remaining sets of threes and invited them to do the same. She walked among the discussion groups listening for the first lull and then signalled closure.

TEACHER: When I count to five, please end your conversations. 1-2-3-4-5. Is there someone willing to share his or her experience with us?

The count allows some time for closure.

Silence blanketed the earlier noisy room. The teacher waited for a reluctant hand.

It is much easier to encourage talk in a small group than in a large one.

TEACHER: Thank you. What experiences did people in your group have that built up their self-esteem?

PARENTS: One woman's boss acknowledged her obvious competence and commented on what a smart person she was.

I have lost 29 pounds and my friends are noticing. I feel so great I plan to stay like this.

TEACHER: What were the critical elements that caused the esteem to grow?

Retrieving the gems from the stories makes explicit what makes a difference.

PARENTS: Honest comments.

Amount of effort was worthy of praise.

Acknowledgment.

Sincerity.

The effort was acknowledged, not the result.

Timing.

TEACHER: Number ones stand and move to another number one spot. This time in your group think of a time when you noticed someone else's self-esteem grow. You didn't have anything to do with the growth. You just watched it happen. You were the witness. What caused it to happen?

After three or four minutes she began counting to signal closure.

TEACHER: 1, 2, 3, 4, 5. Thank you. What did you notice about your thinking this time?

Rather than asking for retelling, the teacher focuses on the group processes and metacognition, thus encouraging more transfer.

PARENTS: It was a little tricky to think as an outsider.

I went back to my childhood and thought of my sisters.

TEACHER: Did you notice anything about your group this time?

PARENT: The first time we were all a little reluctant. This time we all started talking at once.

TEACHER: What did you notice about your own feelings?

PARENT: At first I felt annoyed because I came to hear a lecture on self-concept. I wanted to hear what to do for my child. Now I am enjoying the sharing.

TEACHER: My goal in this strategy is to show that we all really know the bottom line on confidence building. What we have to do is build on what works. Near the end of the session we will have things that we all can do. Who will share an experience of watching someone's self-esteem grow?

PARENT: My son gets really upset when his father goes to work. My husband had a chat one night with him and gave Jeff his business card with permission to phone him at the office when he gets lonesome. You should have seen him beam!

TEACHER: What critical element is playing here?

PARENTS: The adult is responding to the child's need in a meaning-ful way.

The child has been treated with the message "You are important so you can call me."

The adults are constructing their personal meaning from sharing thinking about group experiences.

TEACHER: Would someone else like to share an experience?

PARENT: Well, our five-year-old was being really hard on herself about her ballet lessons. She kept saying, "I am dumb. I can't do it." My husband took time off work and went to her class to watch. He found many instances where he could say, "I know some of the steps were hard, but I saw you. . . ." She turned on her heel and said, "I like ballet, Daddy." All she needed was for him to see some-thing positive to help her.

TEACHER: What were the critical elements here?

PARENTS: Seeing something that matched what she knew, so that the authentic feedback at the right moment built her con-fidence.

Stressing the positive.

Sincerity and tone of voice.

Valuing her enough to take time off work to build up her confidence.

TEACHER: Thank you. Now number twos stand and move to a new spot. This time think of a time when you planned or caused some-one's self-esteem to grow. What did you do and why did it work? You have four minutes.

A time allotment is imposed once the participants are more engaged with the process.

130

After the four minutes she stopped them with the familiar, 1, 2, 3, 4, 5. The groups reflected experiences that caused others to feel good about themselves.

TEACHER: I am hearing such thoughtful ways of building up others. Would anyone like to share how he or she helped someone's self-esteem grow?

PARENT: Two nights ago I was desperate. Company was coming in an hour and I had computer paper and reference books spread all over the room. I turned to our eight-year-old son and said, ''I need your help.'' He helped me restore order without a word. I realized that we needed to involve him in more responsibility because typically I would have fussed and done it all myself. His self-esteem was boosted by being needed and taking charge.

TEACHER: We've looked at self-esteem from three perspectives now: first, as a personal experience; second, as a witness; and third, as a person planning to boost someone's self-esteem. Number threes move this time. In your groups make a list of some of the key factors that influence self-esteem.

The teacher reviews the process to clarify before giving further instructions.

The participants huddled in conversation again, building details from the discussion.

The participants are actively constructing understanding and making action plans.

PARENTS: Listening to another person, looking into that person's eyes.

Positive, encouraging comments.

Stressing strengths, not weaknesses.

Opportunities for a person to take responsibility and feel a part of the action.

Feedback from a peer.

The 'group share' presents more examples for all to hear and recognizes the expertise of the adults present.

TEACHER: If you had one piece of advice for a friend, what would you say?

Highlighting one piece personalizes each participant's most salient point.

PARENTS: Remember to treat children the way you'd like to be treated.

Give kids responsibilities that you know they can accomplish.

Give them the satisfaction of being successful.

Encourage their efforts more than their results.

TEACHER: Let's reflect for a moment. Why would I choose this strategy with this topic?

The teacher models for the parents how learning works in today's classrooms.

PARENTS: It forced us to get inside our own experiences and share.

   To make us feel good about ourselves.

   To keep us all involved.

   To make us work.

TEACHER: What did you notice about your thinking as we worked in different groups?

PARENTS: I was nervous at first.

   I wasn't sure what you were after. Once we got going, I liked the little groups. I usually don't think of myself as liking group work.

TEACHER: As teachers work with important curriculum concepts, they use this strategy to find out what the children know or to deepen understandings or to help them become part of a social and a learning group. Thank you for your participation this evening. I have brought you a few suggestions, many of which you have already mentioned, that you can do at home. Perhaps reading these handouts will spark new ways to build your child's self-esteem.

An additional short hand-out extends the learning and after the interaction, moves beyond 'one right answer'.

Extensions

1. *Primary level theme on friends:*

   Think of a time when you helped someone.
   Think of a time when you saw someone being helped.
   Think of a time when you caused someone to help someone else.

2. *Social studies on the Gold Rush:*

   Think of a time when you were given an opportunity.
   Think of a time when you noticed someone getting an opportunity.
   Think of a time when you planned or caused someone to have an opportunity.

3. *Spelling strategy building:*

   Think of a time when you spelled a difficult word correctly. What did you do?
   Think of a time when you saw someone spell a difficult word correctly. What did you see that person do?
   Think of a time when you helped someone spell a difficult word. What did you do?

THINK OF A TIME 1, 2, 3: RECIPE

1. Students are grouped in threes.

2. Students are instructed to "think of a time when. . ." around a topic and share their thinking with their small group.

3. The first "think of a time" is as a participant — when it happened to you or you were the actor.

4. After the small-group exchange and the class sharing, one student moves to join a new group.

5. The second "think of a time" is as a witness — when you saw. . . .

6. After the small-group exchange and the class sharing, the second student from each group moves to find a new group.

7. The third "think of a time" is as a causal agent — when you planned or caused to happen. . . .

8. Again, after exchanging views in the small group and in the large one, students return to their original triad.

9. Teacher helps isolate the critical learning variables which have been shared.

10. Students reflect on the process in their triads.

11. Students reflect personally.

14

Learning Logs

One of the greatest changes in our teaching is the time we now spend in reflection — alone, with our colleagues, and with our students. *Learning Logs* presents samples from early primary through the grades which invite you to include your students in 'thinking about their thinking' in both process and content. Suggestions for learning log entries are given for beginning the lesson, in the middle of the lesson, and at the end of the lesson — to consolidate, review, extend, and personalize learning.

"The Teaching About Thinking, what is properly called 'metacognition' or 'going beyond thinking', may be the most powerful and important of all approaches. First, it is the glue that binds all the pieces. . . . Metacognitive activity encourages the skillful thinker to make the connections with conscious effort. Secondly, metacognition is a critical part of the process whereby the student masters any of the thinking skills."

— James Bellanca and Robin Fogarty, *Catch Them Thinking.*

"Effective Evaluation . . . considers the processes and strategies students use to become independent readers and, in so doing, takes into account their ability to select, implement, and evaluate appropriate strategies from a growing repertoire."

— Sharon Jeroski, Faye Brownlie, and Linda Kaser, *Reading and Responding.*

"The journal can be used for academic deliberation, for personal response, and for self-examination. The mode is flexible, allowing for individual differences in purpose and response to surface."

— Sheilah Allen, "Writing to Learn: The Use of the Journal."

"Writing reactions in learning logs helps both teachers and students become more strategic about their approaches to learning. This writing experience offers time for reflection on what works best and helps them evolve their own effective systems for learning."

— Reading/Language in Secondary School Subcommittee of IRA, "Classroom Action Research: The teacher as researcher."

One of the most powerful tools for enabling students to gain more control of their learning is the **Learning Log**. Essentially, this is a reflective journal, often called a Brain Book, which is used at various times during the learning sequence to plan, to reflect on what has been learned and on how it has been learned, to comment on one's thinking, to comment on participation in individual, collaborative or whole class activities, and to personally question what else the learner needs to know in order to achieve understanding.

Logs are often kept in half-size exercise books, in half and half (lined and unlined) exercise books, in separate notebooks, or in a separate part of a binder. However, some teachers find it useful to have students reflect on their learning right on the assignment.

Writing in a learning log is not time consuming. A reflective entry often takes only five minutes. It is followed by sharing one's thinking with a partner, or by a brief whole class sharing, enabling the teacher to extend the students' thinking and to make connections and applications.

Learning logs are not taken in for marking. Feedback helps students develop the language of reflection and gain control over their learning, but this strategy is not 'done for marks'.

As we spend more time reflecting in and on learning, we notice dramatic increases in students' abilities to articulate and achieve metacognitive control over themselves as learners. This conscious use of time for comment by students on themselves as active learners is new to many of us and to our students. The experience often feels quite different when we first begin ''stepping outside our brains and looking back in at what is happening''. Our personal experience is to persevere because the impact on creating independent learners, who have the ability to make learning work for them, is significant.

Students of all ages benefit from self-reflection. The reflective writing allows students to distance themselves from their learning and gain a perspective on it. It also enables them to become more independent, to share in the instructional decisions made in the classroom, and learn to self-evaluate.

Some early primary teachers choose to reflect with their students on chart paper at the end of a strategy. The collection of student thoughts is recorded and makes a visible record of student thinking. Prior to using the strategy again, the class can review their reflections and notice how they can build on their thinking. Then, after the strategy, the class can again reflect and add new thoughts to the growing record, in a different color of pen.

Fran Gamache of Gibsons implemented **Learning Logs** with her early primary class for the first time this year. In sharing the following samples with us she mentioned keeping a personal learning log to help monitor and direct her change process. Fran keeps track of the strategies she uses, what she liked and didn't like about her presentations, and gives advice to herself on improvements or directions for the next time. Fran notices that her five- and six-year-olds are building on each others' responses as they reflect on these metacognitive questions. In September, the children generated reasons for wanting to read. This list has been posted and, as children achieve a personal reading goal, they check off their success on the class list.

WHY I WANT TO READ

- in case I get lost
- to make a special card
- to read my address
- to read directions
- to use computers
- to read the calendar
- to read signs on the road
- to read other peoples' names
- to read color words
- to read my mail

Another use of the **Class Learning Log** is in developing criteria. Fran's children reflected on what made story maps interesting, after they had made their own story maps out of a variety of materials. As the children volunteered their ideas, Fran used this opportunity to extend their language. For example, ''I like all the little things that Jon put in his picture'' became ''details''.

WHAT MAKES A GOOD MAP?

- detail
- use of color
- different ideas for making things such as bridges
- use of different materials (blocks, pasticine, lego)
- a path to show where the characters went

This reflection is now on display for review and future reference by the children.

A third use of the **Class Learning Log** is in addressing the challenges that children are encountering as they break into reading and writing. Identifying and acknowledging that which is personally difficult allows us to develop social support networks in the classroom and to celebrate personal achievements.

WHAT DO YOU FIND HARD ABOUT WRITING IN YOUR DIARY?

- Jason has a hard time sounding the words.
- Anthony says it is starting to get easy.
- Bobby sometimes finds it confusing because his dad told him that sometimes the 'y' sounds like 'e'.
- Anthony says when he hears an 'e' at the end of a word he puts a 'y'.

Nellie Gray, also of Gibsons, has also begun using **Learning Logs** this year with her Grade 2s and 4s. Nellie reflects that as a teacher she needed to be at a certain level of readiness in order to begin to implement learning logs on a regular basis. Since establishing this as a personal goal and forming a Friday share group with two other teachers to discipline themselves, continue commitment, and share progress with one another, she is enthusiastic with the many uses she has found and with the students' ease in writing about their thinking and learning. She now thinks that student self-evaluation is the most valuable strategy of all. When her students are actively participating in evaluating their work, they are assuming a greater degree of responsibility for the quality of work that they do. The learning log is tying the 'fun' of the strategies to the 'business' of learning. Nellie's students have personal exercise books for their logs. They write individually, then share their responses in order to learn about how the other students are thinking and to listen to the language they use to express this thinking.

In October, Nellie asked her Grade 2 students to cluster in their learning logs what they knew about the Namib desert.

Learning Log Entry — Namib Desert Cluster (Grade 2)

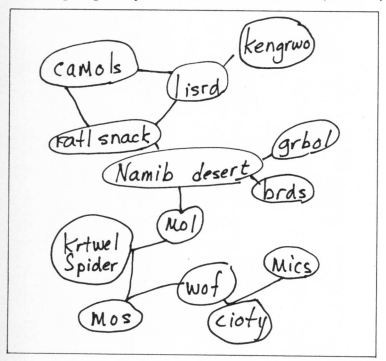

In November, Nellie made little photocopied signs which the students chose and pasted in their learning logs as prompts.

TEACHER: [**Recall Direction**—Grade 2] Tell me in your learning logs what you remember about the story ''A River Dream.''

STUDENTS: We have read the story about a boy that likes fishing so his uncle gave him a box of flys he went fishing in his uncles bout he did not no it and met his uncle woch told him it was his bout.

TEACHER: **[Sort and Classify**—Grade 2] What did you find out about your thinking when you did this exercise?

STUDENT: I was thinking harder it was a little hard for me.

TEACHER: **[Sponge**—Grade 2] List three or more topics that we reviewed this morning in math class.

STUDENTS: We did math pages 54 56 57.

> We did free time.
>
> It was fun.
>
> We made a cube.
>
> We worked with echuther and saw if the cube slided.

Learning Log Entries (Grade 4)

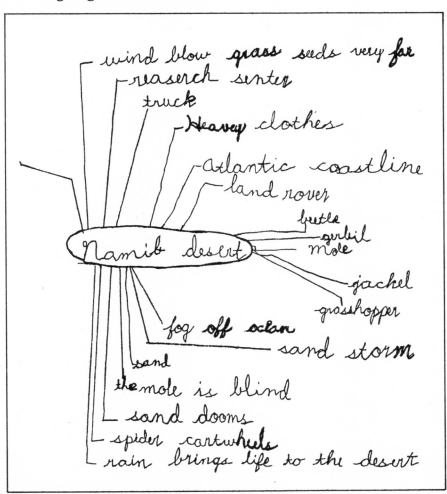

Namib desert
1989-10-18

The Namib desert is full of wildlife like any other desert. All kinds of insects live there, there is also a wide variety of lizards. No one nows how all the sand got there. The jackel is a menice to farmers. The closer to the seawater the hotter it is. In the daytime it's hot, in the night it's freezing.

Recall — Tell me about what we have read in the story, A River Dream.

1989-11-2 e

In 1909 in a desert 6 aciologist's discoverd the ancient tomb

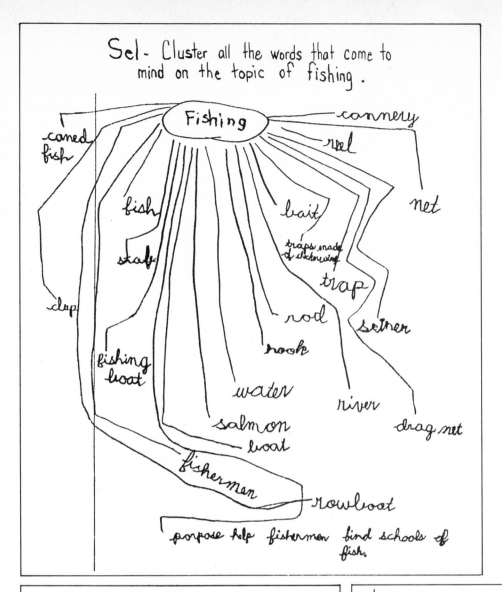

Sel - Cluster all the words that come to mind on the topic of fishing.

Fishing

cannery
reel
net
caned fish
fish
bait
traps made of chicken wire
trap
staff
seiner
clap
rod
hook
fishing boat
water
river
drag net
salmon
boat
fisherman
rowboat

purpose help fisherman find schools of fish.

The ~~Witch~~ Witch

1989-12-01

The Witch was about a witch who kept on kidnapping kids; by leaving a trail of toys leading to ~~her~~ her house. She was going to eat the children but they ~~got~~ away. The children

---

1989-12-20   To improve

I could not go so fast I could study more I could ignore people who talk to me.

Sometimes it is advantageous to have the children reflect on their thinking right on the assignment or on the back of the paper.

The following samples are a first-time reflection for this group of students, after their initial exposure to the strategy **Thinking Boxes**, using the Dayal Kaur Khalsa's text, *I Want a Dog*. The students were asked to step outside their brains and notice what had been happening during the afternoon. The variety of responses which this group of Grade 2 children gave is reflective of their personal styles:

Learning Log Entries (Grade 2)

This afternoon I had lots of fun and I'm saying thank you for coming into our class and picking us to teach. I learned how May actted like when she wanted a dog and that you will never get a dog when you act like that.
— love the Elementary G. 2 class.

Dange - 7years

Today when you read a book about dogs it made me think of my dog because my dog ran away. I felt sad. But the story made me feel good. It made me think of my dog. My dog was small and cuddly. I liked my dog. When I first got my dog I was happy very happy.

Lori, 7years

I was going back in my head about the story.
It was hard to do it but I did it.

This is a good conclution

Tom - 7

I ⁴got all of my idas from the story

and I thinking. I thought all about the story

for about 1min. I thought if I took my

time I could think of something. I'm glad I
thought of these answers. I am glad you picked our
class.

Kim - 7years

Ron McLean of Burnaby has developed a response sheet which he uses with his intermediate students in math. Ron uses these sheets to help his students consolidate their understandings, to focus on application and transfer, and to think about their thinking.

Response Sheet - Math

Name Melanie

Response Sheet

I. **What I Know:**

I know how to estimate.
You guess how many beans are in a jar
Well so like a guess
Odin multiplycation you can estimate the answer

II. **Thinking About New Learning:**

I learned how to front end truncating,
multiply and estimate at the same
time. First you look at the number

III. **Reflecting on Learning:**

1. **What I now know**

I know how to front end trunkating
Muuliply and estimate at the same time

2. **Questions I still have**

no questions

3. **What I noticed about my thinking**

When you consentrate you get tired

Response Sheet   Math

Name Carolyn

Response Sheet

I. **What I Know:** Estimating is like a good
guess it can be used in all different
ways. It can help you in alot of ways
by rounding off the the numbers estimate
them times and get your answer.

II. **Thinking About New Learning:**

I learned that if you round off and estimate
you have a better chance of getting the
question right. I learned in multipication
that you can round off numbers that
do with multipication   ⟶

III. **Reflecting on Learning:**

1. **What I now know** I now know how, use estimater and
multiplacation at the same time

2. **Questions I still have**

3. **What I noticed about my thinking**

I noticed that if you really consantrate
you can do better

$$\begin{array}{r} +\ 798761 \\ +\ 187542 \\ \hline 1\,000\,000 \end{array}$$

The **Learning Log** is typically used at the beginning of a lesson as a focus or anticipatory set, in the middle of the lesson to consolidate, question, or review, or at the end of the lesson as a wraparound. Some teachers have found the following prompts helpful:

TO BEGIN

- What questions do you have from yesterday?
- Write two important points from yesterday's lesson.
- Write two questions that you could now answer.
- Explain. . . .
- Explain in a memo, to someone who was not here, what we learned yesterday.
- Think of a way to use _____ since we practised it in class.

IN THE MIDDLE

- What do you know now?
- What do you want to know more about?
- How is this like something else?
- Cluster what you know on this topic.
- What do you notice about your thinking?
- Is this easy or hard for you? Explain why.
- Connect this to something you know well.
- What advice would you give me before we continue the lesson?
- Sketch what you now know.

AT THE END

- Something I heard which surprised me. . . .
- Someone who helped my thinking. . . .
- Something I will do differently next time. . . .
- Something I am doing better now than before. . . .
- A summary.
- What problems do you still have?
- What strategies did you use?
- What was the best example of your thinking today?
- Explain how your thinking was different today from yesterday — from what it will be tomorrow.
- How will you use this outside of class?
- Who do you know that would find this learning (content) or strategy (process) helpful?
- Reflect on the strategy we used and why we used it.
- Reflect on a conversation you had which triggered your thinking.
- Reflect on something you observed which triggered your thinking.

- I helped move my group's thinking forward because. . . .
- The group helped my thinking because. . . .
- My group worked well because. . . .
- Advice we can work on is. . . .
- An example of collaboration today was. . . .
- An example of something we did better collaboratively than we could have done individually. . . .

Bibliography

Albert, Linda. *A Teacher's Guide to Cooperative Discipline*. Circle Pines, Minnesota: American Guidance Service, 1989.

A Legacy for Learners. *The Report of the Royal Commission on Education*. Victoria, B.C.: Queen's Printer, III, 1988.

Allen, Sheilah. *Writing to Learn: The Use of the Journal. Reading Around Series*, ed. Dr. Fred Gollasch. Carlton, Victoria: Australian Reading Association, 3. September 1989.

Anderson, Valerie and Suzaqnne Hidi. ''Teaching Students to Summarize.'' *Educational Leadership*: 46: 26-28. January 1989.

Andrews, Richard. Presentation at the Enhancing School Quality Conference, Vancouver, B.C., 1989.

Arlin, Patricia. ''Stages of Knowing: A Continuum.'' Opening Address, New Beginnings Conference, University of British Columbia, Vancouver, B.C. May 1989.

Barrs, Myra, Sue Ellis, Hilary Hester, and Anne Thomas. *The Primary Language Record*. Markham, Ontario: Pembroke Publishers, 1988.

Bereiter, C. and M. Scardamalia. ''From Conversation to Composition: The Role of Instruction in a Developmental Process.'' In *Advances in Instructional Psychology*. Vol. 2., ed. R. Glaser. Hillsdale, New Jersey: Bribaum, 1982.

Bolton, R. *People Skills*. Sydney: Simon and Schuster, 1987.

Brandt, Ron. ''On Philosophy in the Curriculum: A Conversation with Matthew Lipman.'' *Educational Leadership*: 46: 34-37. September 1988.

Bransford, J.D. *Human Condition: Learning, Understanding and Remembering*. Belmont, California: Wadsworth, 1979.

Bransford, John D., M. Susan Bums, Victor R. Delclos, and Nancy J. Vye. ''Teaching Thinking. Evaluating Evaluations and Broadening the Data Base''. *Educational Leadership*: 44: 68-70. October 1986.

Bromley, Karen D'Angelo. ''Buddy journals make the reading-writing connection.'' *The Reading Teacher*: 12-129. November 1989.

Brownlie, Faye. ''The Door Is Open. Won't You Come In?'' In *Opening the Door to Classroom Research*, ed. Mary W. Olson. Newark, Delaware: International Reading Association, 1990.

Brownlie, Faye, Susan Close, and Linda Wingren. *Reaching for Higher Thought*. Edmonton, Alberta: Arnold Publishing Ltd., 1988.

Canfield, Jack and Harold C. Wells. *100 Ways to enhance self-concept in the classroom*. Englewood Cliffs, New Jersey: Prentice-Hall Inc., 1976.

Chang, G.L. and C.G. Wells. "The literate potential of collaborative talk." In *Oracy Matters*, M. MacLure, T. Phillips, and A. Wilkinson, eds. Stony Stratford: Open University Press, 1988.

Close, Susan and Sheila Borman. *Reading Like An Expert*. Prime Areas: British Columbia Teachers' Federation: 61-65. Fall 1988.

Collins, Allen, John Seely Brown, and Susan E. Newman. *Cognitive Apprenticeship: Teaching the Craft of Reading, Writing and Mathematics*. Champaign, Illinois: University of Illinois Centre for the Study of Reading, Technical Report, No. 403. 1987.

Courtenay, Richard. *Re-Cognizing Richard Courtenay: Selected Writings on Drama and Education*. Markham, Ontario: Pembroke Publishers, 1988.

Crowell, Sam. "A New Way of Thinking: The Challenge of the Future." *Educational Leadership*: 60-63. September 1989.

Curwin, Richard L. *Discipline with Dignity*. Alexandria, Virginia: Association for Supervision and Curriculum Development, 1990.

Dalton, Joan. *Adventures in Thinking*. Melbourne, Australia: Nelson, 1985.

Davidson, Jane L. and Bonnie C. Wilkerson. *Directed Reading-Thinking Activities*. Monroe, New York: Trillium Press, 1988.

Derry, Sharon J. "Putting Learning Strategies to Work." *Educational Leadership*: 46:4-10. December/January, 1988/1989.

Dwyer, Barry, ed. "A Sea of Talk." Rozelle, N.S.W.: Primary English Teaching Association. February 1989.

Dwyer, Barry. "Parents Teachers Partners". Rozelle, N.S.W.: Primary English Teaching Association. February 1989.

Elbow, Peter. *Embracing Contraries*. New York: Oxford University Press, 1986.

Fox, Nancy V. "Providing Effective Inservice Education." *Journal of Reading*: 33: 214-215.

Fulwiler, Toby. "Writing and Learning, Grade Three." *Language Arts*: 55-59 (62). 1985.

Gall, Meredith. "Synthesis of Research on Teachers' Questioning." *Educational Leadership*: 45:25-30. November 1984.

Glickman, Carl. "Unlocking school reform: Uncertainty as a condition of professionalism." *Phi Delta Kappan*: 120-122. October 1987.

Green, Vicki A. "Creating an Environment for Literacy – Intermediate." A Paper Presented at the Whole Language Institute, University of Victoria, Victoria, B.C. August 1989.

Hart, Leslie A. *Human Brain and Human Learning*. New Rochelle, New York: Brain Age Publishers, 1983.

Hillocks, George Jr. "Synthesis of Research on Teaching Writing." *Educational Leadership*: 71-81. May 1987.

Hord, Shirley M., Williams L. Rutherford, Leslie Huling-Austin, and Gene E. Hall. *Taking Charge of Change*. Alexandria, Virginia: ASCD, 1987.

Jeroski, Sharon. "Reading Achievement: Beginning to Make Sense." Prime Areas: British Columbia Teachers' Federation, 12-14. Fall 1989.

Jeroski, Sharon, Faye Brownlie, and Linda Kaser. *Reading and Responding: Evaluation Resources for Teachers*. Scarborough: Nelson Canada, 1990.

Johnson, David W. and Roger T. Johnson. *Leading the Cooperative School*. Edina, Minnesota: Interaction Book Company, 1989.

Johnson, Peter. "Teachers as evaluation experts." *Reading Teacher*: 744-748. April 1987.

Johnson, Terry D. and Daphne R. Louis. *Bringing It All Together*. Richmond Hill, Ontario: Scholastic, 1990.

Jones, Beau Fly, Jean Pierce, and Barbara Hunter. "Teaching Students to Construct Graphic Representations." *Educational Leadership:* 20-25. January 1989.

Joyce, Bruce, Beverly Showers, and Carol Rolheiser-Bennett. "Staff Development and Student Learning: A Synthesis of Research on Models of Teaching." *Educational Research*: 45: 17–23. October 1987.

Kelly-Smith, Linda. "Role Drama as a Process for Promoting Self-Esteem." Prime Areas: British Columbia Teachers' Federation: 59-61. Winter 1989.

Kingman, J. *Report of the Committee of Inquiry into the Teaching of the English Language*. London: H.M.S.O., 1988.

Lambert, L. "Staff Development Redesigned." *Phi Delta Kappan*: 71-82. May 1988.

Macrorie, Ken. *20 Teachers*. New York: Oxford University Press, 1984.

Marzano, Robert J. and Daisy E. Arrendondo. *Tactics for Thinking*. Aurora, Colorado: Mid-Continent Regional Educational Laboratory, 1986.

Marzano, Robert J., Ronald S. Brandt, Carolyn Sue Hughes, Beau Fly Jones, Barbara Z. Presseisen, Stuart C. Rankin, and Charles Suhor. *Dimensions of Thinking: A Framework for Curriculum and Instruction*. Alexandria, Virginia. Association for the Supervision of Curriculum Development, 1988.

Marx, Ronald and Tarrance Grieve. *The Learners of British Columbia*. Commissioned Papers: Volume 2. British Columbia Royal Commission on Education. May 1988.

McGinley, William and Robert J. Tierney. *Reading and Writing as Ways of Knowing and Learning*. Champaign, Illinois: University of Illinois Center for the Study of Reading. Technical Report No. 423. April 1988.

McLaren, Milton. *A Curricular Perspective on the Principle of Understanding Curriculum: Towards Developing a Common Understanding*, ed. Ronald W. Marx. Victoria, B.C.: Ministry of Education. September 1989.

McClure, Michael F. "Collaborative Learning: Teacher's Game or Students' Game?" *English Journal:* 66-68. February 1990.

McKim, Robert H. *Thinking Visually*. Palo Alto, California: Dale Seymour Publications, 1990.

McTighe, Jay and Frank T. Lyman, Jr. "Cueing Thinking in the Classroom: The Promise of Theory-Embedded Tools." *Educational Leadership* 45:18-24. April 1988.

Mickelson, Norma. "Recasting evaluation: centred in the classroom." *Teacher*: 11-12. December 1989.

Monahan, Joy and Beth Hinson, project directors. *New Directions in Reading Instruction.* Newark, Delaware: International Reading Association, 1988.

National Curriculum Council. *English for Ages 5 to 16.* York, England. Department of Education and Science and the Welsh Office. June 1989.

Neubert, G.A. and E.C. Bratton. "Team Coaching: Staff Development Side by Side." *Educational Leadership:* 29-32. February 1987.

Newkirk, Thomas. *More Than Stories: The Range of Children's Writing.* Portsmouth, New Hampshire: Heinemann, 1989.

Novak, Joseph D. and Bob D. Gowin. *Learning How to Learn.* New York: Cambridge University Press, 1984.

Ogle, Donna M. "Implementing Strategic Teaching." *Education Leadership:* 47-60. January 1989.

Palincsar, A.S. and A.L. Brown. "Interactive teaching to promote independent learning from text." *The Reading Teacher:* 771-777. 1986.

Panincsar, Annemarie, Kathryn Ransom, and Sue Derber. "Collaborative Research and Development of Reciprocal Teaching." *Educational Leadership:* 37-40. January 1989.

Parsons, Les. *Response Journals.* Markham, Ontario: Pembroke Publishers, 1989.

Raphael, T.E. and J. McKinney. "An Examination of Fifth and Eighth-Grade Children's Question-Answering Behavior: An Instructional Study in Metacognition." *Journal of Reading Behavior,* 15:67-86. 1983.

Reeves, Noelene. *Children Writing Maths. Reading Around Series,* ed. Dr. Fred Gollasch. Carlton, Victoria: Australian Reading Association, 3. August 1988.

Reid, Jo-Anne, Peter Forrestal, and Jonathan Cook. *Small Group Learning in the Classroom.* Rozelle, N.S.W., Primary English Teaching Association: Chalkface Press, 1989.

Resnick, Lauren B. and Leopold E. Klopfer. "Toward the Thinking Curriculum: Concluding Remarks". In *Toward the Thinking Curriculum: Current Cognitive Research.* Alexandria, Virginia: ASCD, 1989.

Rico, Gabriele Lusser. "Daedalus and Icarus Within: The Literature/Art/Writing Connection." *English Journal:* Vol. 78, No. 3: 14-23. March 1989.

Samples, Bob. *Open Mind: Whole Mind.* Rolling Hills Estates, California: Jalmar Press, 1987.

Santa, Carol M. "Teaching As Research." In *Opening the Door to Classroom Research,* ed. Mary W. Olson. Newark, Delaware: International Reading Association, 1990.

Spiro, Rand J., W.P. Vispoel, John G. Schmitz, Ala Samarapungavan, and A.E. Boerger. *Knowledge Acquisition for Application: Cognitive Flexibility and Transfer in Complex Content Domains.* Urbana, Illinois: University of Illinois Centre for the Study of Reading, Technical Report, No. 409. September 1987.

Stauffer, Russell. *Teaching Reading as a Thinking Process.* New York: Harper and Row, 1969.

Steele, Bob. *Credo*. Drawing Network Newsletter #3. Vancouver, B.C.: University of British Columbia.

Strong, Richard, Harvey F. Silver, and Robert Hanson. "New Strategies, New Visions." *Educational Leadership*: October 1986, pp. 52-54.

Swartz, Larry. *Dramathemes: A Practical Guide for Teaching Drama.* Markham, Ontario: Pembroke Publishers, 1988.

Tierney, Robert J. "Redefining Reading Comprehension." *Educational Leadership:* 37-42. March 1990.

vos Savant, Marilyn. *Brain Building*. New York, New York: Bantam Books, 1990.

Wells, Gordon, Gen Ling M. Chang and Ann Maher (in press). "Creating Classroom Communities of Literate Thinkers." In *Cooperative Learning: Theory and Research*, S. Sharon, ed. New York, New York: Praeger.

Willis, Scott. "Feeling Good and Doing Well." *ASCD Update*. Alexandria, Virginia. March 1990.

Wilson, Marilyn. "Critical Literacy/Critical Thinking." *Language Arts*, Vol. 65, No. 6. October 1988.

Winograd and Scott G. Paris. "A Cognitive and Motivational Agenda for Reading Instruction." *Educational Leadership:* 30-35. January 1989.

Yaffe, Stephen H. "Drama as a Teaching Tool." *Educational Leadership:* 29-32. March 1989.

Zola, Melanie. *Story Drama: A Window to the World of Whole Language*. British Columbia Teachers' Federation: 80-85. Fall 1988.

Student Response Sheet

Strategy: Retelling and Predicting

Name: _____ Date: _____

Retelling	Prediction
	_____ _____ _____ _____ _____ _____ _____ _____ _____
	_____ _____ _____ _____ _____ _____ _____ _____ _____
	_____ _____ _____ _____ _____ _____ _____ _____

Teacher Observation Form

Strategy: Editing Persuasion

Name: _____   Date/s: _____

Interaction	Draft 1	Draft 2	Draft 3

Comments: _____
_____
_____
_____
_____

Teacher Observation Form

Strategy: Editing Description

Name: _____ Date/s: _____

Interaction	Draft 1	Draft 2	Draft 3

Comments: _____
_____
_____
_____
_____

Teacher Observation Form

Strategy: Editing a Story

Name: _____ Date/s: _____

Interaction	Draft 1	Draft 2	Draft 3

Comments: _____

_____

_____

_____

_____

Teacher Observation Form

Strategy: Listen-Sketch-Draft

Date/s: _____

Student	Interaction — with partner — with class	Sketching	Summarizing	Reflections

Comments: _____
_____
_____
_____
_____

Student Response Sheet

Strategy: Listen-Sketch-Draft

Name: _____   Date: _____

Prediction:

	1.
	2.
	3.
	What I noticed about my thinking.